Fishes of the Minnesota Region

*The University of Minnesota Press
gratefully acknowledges the assistance
for publication provided by
Wallace C. and Mary Lee Dayton.*

Fishes
of the
Minnesota Region

Gary L. Phillips
William D. Schmid
James C. Underhill

UNIVERSITY OF MINNESOTA PRESS
Minneapolis

Library of Congress Cataloging in Publication Data

Phillips, Gary L.
  Fishes of the Minnesota region.

  Bibliography: p.
  Includes index.
  1. Fishes — Minnesota. I. Schmid, William D.   II. Underhill, James
Campbell   II. Title.
QL628.M6P47   597.092'9776   81-14693
ISBN 0-8166-0979-9   AACR2
ISBN 0-8166-0982-9 (pbk.)

DEDICATION

To Samuel Eddy, teacher, and John B. Moyle,
scientist, who were friends to
their colleagues and to the fishes they knew so well.

TABLE OF CONTENTS

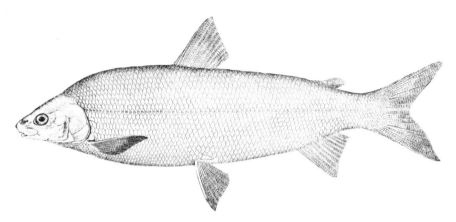

Lake whitefish. From United States Commission of Fish and Fisheries. 1884. Washington, D.C.: *The Fisheries and Fishery Industries of the United States.*

Northern pike as depicted by a nineteenth-century artist. From Henry William Herbert. 1864. *Frank Forester's Fish and Fishing of the United States and British Provinces of North America.* New York: W. A. Townsend.

PREFACE

This book was written for all who are interested in fishes and would like to know more about them. Its main objectives are to acquaint the reader with the fishes that live in Minnesota and to show why they are important. In this guide to 149 kinds of fishes, brief discussions of their classifications, distributions, and life histories are given; 88 kinds are illustrated in color photographs.

All fishes discussed in this guide are found in Minnesota. Because many of them are in waters outside the state as well, readers in adjacent areas should find this book a useful reference.

Most people can accurately identify familiar game fishes, and some fishes, notably the sea lamprey and the carp, are notorious by reputation. Many fishes, however, are less obvious to humans. Because fishes live underwater, we rarely observe them as they normally live, and we understand their ecology only vaguely. All kinds of fishes are worth knowing because each makes its own contribution to the status of the fish population and each is a small but unique part of the natural system in which all organisms, including humans, depend on one another. Fishes are part of the outdoor experience that helps make the Minnesota region a good place in which to live, and they are vitally important to Minnesota's economy. For all these reasons, they deserve care and understanding. We have tried in this book to describe fishes in a way that we hope will stimulate interest in fish watching and add to the enjoyment of angling.

We are grateful to many friends and colleagues whose generous assistance has made this book possible. We thank John Daily, Ed Feiler, Roy Johannes, James Schneider, W. J. Scidmore, and Don Woods, all of the Minnesota Department of Natural Resources, who supplied valuable technical and historical information. Dick Sternberg, formerly of the DNR, provided information and encouragement. Robert Kraske, associate editor of the DNR's *Volunteer* maga-

zine, kindly allowed us to use the article "Cooking Your Catch" for
our section entitled "Fishes as Food."

Dr. David J. Merrell of the University of Minnesota, Dr. Michael
Ross of the University of Massachusetts, and Jeff Holtmeier read
portions of the preliminary draft of this book; Dr. Thomas F. Waters
of the University of Minnesota reviewed the entire manuscript. We
appreciate their many useful suggestions.

We thank Virginia Hollier Pueringer for drawing many of the illus-
trations and Dr. Don Beimborn for contributing color plates showing
various kinds of trouts. Phil Cochran, Tom Coon, Mike Dulski, Mark
Evert, Jay Hatch, Nancy Hurd, Lara Schmid, Robyn Schmid, Chuck
Trinka, and Joe Weinhold all gave willingly of their time and stamina
to help collect the fishes used in photographing the color plates.

G. L. P.
W. D. S.
J. C. U.

Fishes of the Minnesota Region

INTRODUCTION

Each year about 2 million people, 400,000 of them nonresidents, go fishing in Minnesota. Minnesota's anglers might seem peculiar to an objective observer. They drive for miles; they endure cold, rain, wind, balky motors, snags, deerflies, poison ivy, sunburn, and hunger; and then, still not satisfied, they top it off by going to frozen lakes in the winter, chopping holes in the ice, and sitting for hours in "fish houses" — all in the hope of catching a fish. Their optimism is unquenchable: when one day is bad, they are sure the next will be better.

It seems as though any animals that can generate such enthusiasm must have a mystique about them, some irresistible quality. Actually, fishes are so popular simply because they are fun to catch and good to eat.

Minnesota is blessed with a rich fish fauna primarily because it offers fishes plenty of room and a diversity of places to live. Minnesota is said to be the land of 10,000 lakes, but this claim is a modest one. It has been reported that there are 12,034 permanent bodies of standing water in the state. This number is greater than that of any other state, except Alaska. Minnesota also contains about 15,000 linear miles of fishable rivers and streams. The inland lakes and streams of Minnesota cover about 4,900 square miles, which is 6 percent of the state's area. Minnesota's portion of Lake Superior adds another 1,840 square miles. Besides sheer space, Minnesota's waters offer a practically limitless variety of freshwater habitats, from the deep waters of Lake Superior to the shallow waters of prairie lakes, from the North Shore's rushing streams to the sloughs and meandering rivers in the state's forests and prairies. Obviously, there is no mystery in the appeal of fishing to Minnesotans or in their interest in the nature of fishes.

3

Fish Names

In saying that 149 kinds of fishes live in Minnesota, one uses the word "kind" as a synonym for the word "species." Each kind, or species, of plant or animal is a group that maintains an identity separate from all other kinds. Members of a given species can breed freely with each other to produce normal offspring, but they do not breed freely with members of other species. Sometimes, members of different species do interbreed and produce hybrids. Hybridization is somewhat common among certain kinds of fishes. Hybrids are not normal offspring, however, and they are usually sterile.

Each species of plant and animal has two names, one common and one scientific. Walleye is the common name of Minnesota's state fish. The walleye's scientific name is *Stizostedion vitreum*. Although they may be complicated, scientific names are useful, especially to those who study plants and animals. Scientific names are standardized so that a particular species has its own scientific name and no other (discrepancies do occur in special situations, but they need not be considered here). Common names, by contrast, sometimes vary; the walleye, for example, is sometimes called the walleyed pike or the jack salmon, even though it is neither a pike nor a salmon.

The scientific name for a species of plant or animal is usually derived from Latin or Greek words and consists of both a generic (from *genus*, an inclusive group of related species) name and a specific, or trivial, name. The generic name (*Stizostedion*, for example) is capitalized and the specific name (*vitreum*, for example) is not. Each scientific name was assigned by the person who discovered the species, and his or her last name is often given after the scientific name. Most common and scientific names used in this book are those given in the fourth edition of *A List of Common and Scientific Names of Fishes from the United States and Canada* (Robins et al., 1980).

Both the scientific name and the common name usually tell something about the species to which they were given. The name walleye refers, of course, to the large eyes located on the side of the fish's head. *Stizostedion* can be translated as pungent throat; *vitreum* means glass, again in reference to the eyes. In the descriptions of fishes in this book, the common names and the scientific names of all species are given, and the scientific names are translated.

Arrangement of Fishes in This Book

Fishes that are related to each other are grouped into families, such as the minnow family or the sunfish family. Twenty-six families of fishes are represented by at least one species in Minnesota. In the descriptions and portraits section of this book, these families are listed generally from the more primitive to the more advanced. The first family discussed, for example, is the Petromyzontidae, or the lamprey family. Lampreys have neither jaws nor paired fins and are, therefore, reminiscent of the most ancient fishes known. The sequence of families proceeds from the lampreys through to the drums (family Sciaenidae), which, with their **spines, thoracic pelvic fins,** and other specialized characteristics, are structurally highly advanced. (Terms that are defined in the glossary [pages 50–52] are **boldfaced** the first time that they appear in the text.) Within families, the species of fishes are placed in the genus to which they belong, and each is discussed under a heading that gives its scientific and common names.

Aid to Identification of Fishes

The *key* to fishes (page 12) enables one to identify the 26 *families* of Minnesota fishes. A key to all the *species* of Minnesota fishes is beyond the scope of this book, and the reader should consult the third edition of *Northern Fishes* (Eddy and Underhill, 1974) for that key. Some species of fishes (and even some families) resemble each other closely, so caution is needed in making identifications.

The key in this book separates each family of Minnesota fishes from other families on the basis of external characteristics. The key is divided into 25 sets (called couplets) of two contrasting statements. Only one statement in each couplet will fit a particu-

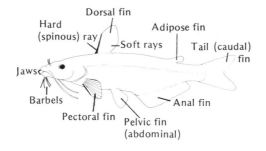

Figure 1. Channel catfish.

lar fish. Always starting with the first couplet, one chooses the statement that fits the fish and proceeds as that statement directs. Keying should be continued until a statement accompanied with an illustration showing *key characteristics* similar to the specimen's is reached. If the key characteristics of the figure and the specimen match, the fish has been keyed to its family. If the key characteristics do not match, a mistake in keying has been made and the procedure must be done over again. Once the fish has been keyed to its family, one can turn to the page number given at the end of the statement to read more about that family and its species. Even though the key in this book does not enable one to key out species, one will be able to identify many species from the descriptions and color plates in the text.

To use the key effectively, one must be familiar with the key characteristics of fishes. Figures 1 and 2, which depict a catfish and a bass, show some structures used to identify fishes. Addi-

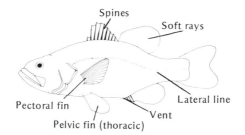

Figure 2. Largemouth bass.

tional characteristics are shown in Figures 3 through 11 and are explained in the accompanying text. Terms pertinent to the key are also included in the glossary.

Jaws

All Minnesota fishes except lampreys have jaws that, although they vary in length and shape, are always obvious (Figure 1). A **larval** (immature) lamprey's mouth is surrounded by a hood (Figure 3), and an adult's mouth is surrounded by a round disc that bears pointed, toothlike structures (Figure 4).

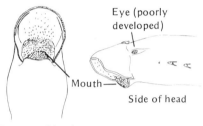

Figure 3. Mouth of immature lamprey.

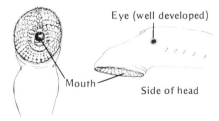

Figure 4. Mouth of mature lamprey.

Paired Fins

The paired fins of fishes are the **pectoral fins** and the pelvic fins. All other fins are unpaired. The pelvic fins are located under the belly in many fishes (that is, they are **abdominal** in position [Figure 1]), but in the course of evolution the pelvic fins of other fishes have moved forward to a position just behind the pectoral fins (thoracic [Figure 2]), or in front of them (**jugular** [Figure 22]).

Lampreys lack paired fins. All other Minnesota fishes have both pectoral and pelvic fins except the American eel, which has pectorals but lacks pelvics. Lampreys and eels resemble each other at first glance, but the presence of jaws and pectoral fins in eels makes identification easy.

Tail (Caudal) Fin

In primitive jawed fishes such as the sturgeons and the paddlefish, the rear tip of the backbone turns upward and causes the upper portion of the **tail (caudal) fin** to be asymmetrical with the lower (Figure 5). This type of tail fin is termed **heterocercal** (*hetero* means unlike). In the gars and the bowfin, the backbone also tips upward, but only slightly, and the tail fin is asymmetrically rounded in adults (Figure 6); therefore, the gars and the bowfin are said to have a modified heterocercal tail fin. All the other jawed fishes in Minnesota have a tail fin in which the lobes are generally symmetrical and the backbone does not extend into either lobe (Figure 1). This type of tail fin is termed **homocercal** (*homo* means like).

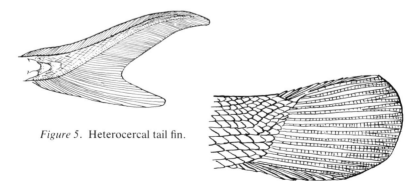

Figure 5. Heterocercal tail fin.

Figure 6. Modified heterocercal tail fin.

Location of Mouth

In some fishes, such as the sturgeons and the paddlefish, the mouth is on the bottom of the head and the snout protrudes far in front of it (Figure 13). A mouth in this location is termed **ventral.** In the other jawed Minnesota fishes, the mouth is at the front of the head and is said to be **terminal** (Figure 1).

Soft Rays, Hard Rays, and Spines

Flexible fin rays, called **soft rays,** are typically jointed and branched. Many Minnesota fishes, such as the trouts, native minnows, and suckers, have only soft rays. Spines are unjointed, unbranched structures found along with soft rays in certain fins of some fishes, such as sunfishes and perches. Spines are usually, but not always, stiff and inflexible. Among Minnesota fishes, the catfishes and two introduced minnows (the carp and the goldfish) have **hard (spinous) rays** that resemble true spines but are jointed and often toothed along the edges (Figure 7).

The number of rays in the **dorsal fin** separates minnows from suckers in the key. The native minnows and the introduced grass carp typically have fewer than 10 dorsal fin rays, usually 8. Most suckers have 12 or considerably more. Two introduced minnows, the carp and the goldfish, also have more than 10. One should fan the dorsal fin when counting its rays and use magnification when necessary. Two standard conventions ap-

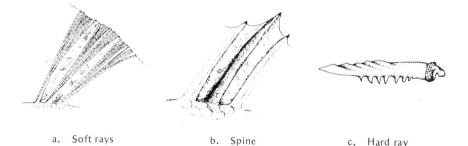

a. Soft rays   b. Spine   c. Hard ray

Figure 7. Examples of (a) soft rays, (b) spine, and (c) hard ray.

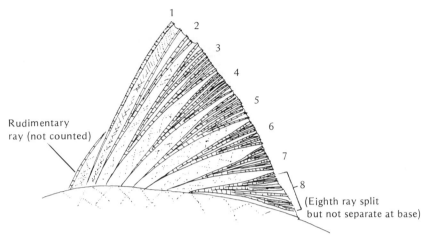

Figure 8. Dorsal fin having eight rays.

ply when one counts rays. First, if the first ray is short and unbranched (rudimentary), it should not be counted (Figure 8). The count should be started with the first long ray, even if it is unbranched. Second, only those rays that are clearly separated from all others at the base should be counted.

Adipose Fin

In addition to all the other fins, some fishes have a fleshy **adipose fin** (adipose means fatty) on the back behind the dorsal fin (Figure 1). It can always be identified by its fleshiness and its lack of supporting rays.

Barbels

Barbels (also called whiskers and feelers) are threadlike, sensory structures located on the heads of some fishes, such as the catfishes (Figure 1).

Pelvic Axillary Processes

The trouts, the mooneyes, and some other fishes have a small, flaplike structure, the **pelvic axillary process,** located near the border of each pelvic fin (Figure 9).

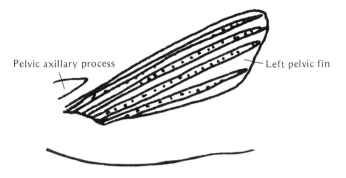

Figure 9. Pelvic axillary process.

Gill Membranes

Except for lampreys, the gills of all Minnesota fishes are covered by a flap, the **operculum.** Along the edge of each operculum is a membrane, the **gill membrane.** The gill membranes are united to the throat under the head. In some fishes, such as the pikes and the mooneyes, the gill membranes attach far forward, under the eye or in front of it (Figure 10). In others, such as the minnows and the suckers, they attach farther back, distinctly behind the eye (Figure 11).

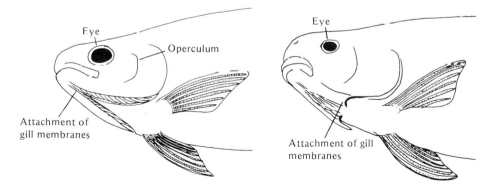

Figure 10. Gill membranes attached under eye.

Figure 11. Gill membranes attached distinctly behind eye.

Lateral Line

A prominent sensory structure in the skin of fishes is the **lateral line,** a series of pores that runs along each side of the body (Figure 2). Some fishes lack a lateral line, and others have an incomplete one that extends partway to the tail fin. The lateral line of the freshwater drum is unique among Minnesota fishes in that it extends all the way through the tail fin.

Vent

The **vent,** or anus, is the opening under the body that terminates the digestive tract. It is typically just in front of the **anal fin** (Figure 2). Early in the life of the pirate perch, however, the vent migrates forward to the throat. This peculiar development distinguishes the pirate perch from all other Minnesota fishes.

Key to Identification of Families of Minnesota Fishes

(Starting with the first pair of terms [couplet], choose which statement fits the fish that you wish to identify. If the statement that you choose ends with a number, go to that number, read the couplet, and continue as directed until you reach a statement that refers you to a figure. Check that figure to see whether the fish shown has the same key characteristics as your fish. If it does, you have keyed out your specimen properly. If it does not, you have made a wrong turn someplace and will have to begin again.)

1a. Jaws and paired fins absent (Figure 12)
. . . . .Lamprey family, Petromyzontidae (page 55)

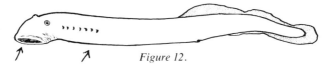

Figure 12.

1b. Jaws and paired fins present . . . . go to 2
2a. Tail fin heterocercal or modified heterocercal. . . . . go to 3
2b. Tail fin homocercal . . . . go to 6

3a. Heterocercal tail forked, mouth ventral . . . . go to 4
3b. Modified heterocercal tail fin rounded, mouth terminal
. . . . go to 5
4a. Snout short, body with bony plates (Figure 13)
. . . . .Sturgeon family, Acipenseridae (page 61)

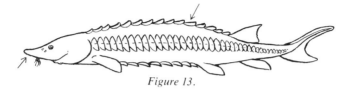

Figure 13.

4b. Snout long and paddlelike, body naked (Figure 14)
. . . . .Paddlefish family, Polyodontidae (page 64)

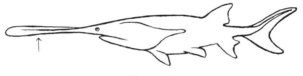

Figure 14.

5a. Jaws long, dorsal fin short (Figure 15)
. . . . .Gar family, Lepisosteidae (page 65)

Figure 15.

5b. Jaws short, dorsal fin long (Figure 16)
. . . . .Bowfin family, Amiidae (page 68)

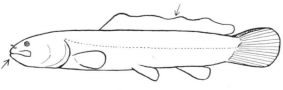

Figure 16.

6a. Pelvic fins absent, body snakelike (Figure 17)
.............Freshwater eel family, Anguillidae (page 75)

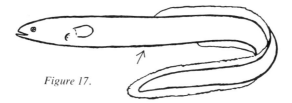

Figure 17.

6b. Pelvic fins present, body not snakelike .... go to 7
7a. Adipose fin present .... go to 8
7b. Adipose fin absent .... go to 11
8a. Barbels present, scales absent (Figure 18)
.... Freshwater catfish family, Ictaluridae (page 170)

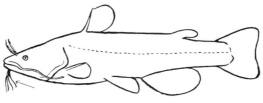

Figure 18.

8b. Barbels absent, scales present .... go to 9
9a. Pelvic axillary processes present (Figure 19)
.................Salmon family, Salmonidae (page 84)

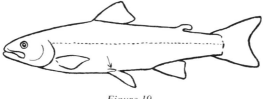

Figure 19.

9b. Pelvic axillary processes absent .... go to 10

10a. Dorsal fin with two weak spines, scales feel rough when rubbed from rear forward (Figure 20)
.... Trout-perch family, Percopsidae (page 181)

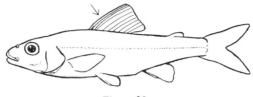

Figure 20.

10b. Dorsal fin without spines, scales feel smooth when rubbed from rear forward (Figure 21)
.... Smelt family, Osmeridae (page 106)

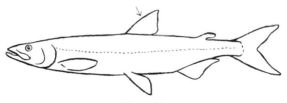

Figure 21.

11a. Barbel on chin (Figure 22)
.... Cod family, Gadidae (page 184)

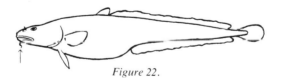

Figure 22.

11b. No barbel on chin............................ go to 12
12a. Scales absent .... go to 13
12b. Scales present................................ go to 14
13a. Dorsal fin preceded by free spines (Figure 23)
.... Stickleback family, Gasterosteidae (page 190)

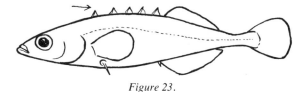

Figure 23.

13b. Dorsal fin spines connected by membranes (Figure 24)
.... Sculpin family, Cottidae (page 193)

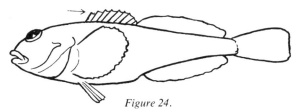

Figure 24.

14a. Pelvic fins abdominal......................... go to 15
14b. Pelvic fins thoracic .... go to 22
15a. Two separate dorsal fins (Figure 25)
.... Silverside family, Atherinidae (page 188)

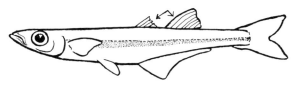

Figure 25.

15b. One dorsal fin .... go to 16
16a. Head scaled or partly scaled................. go to 17
16b. Head without scales......................... go to 19
17a. Jaws duckbill-shaped, tail forked (Figure 26)
........................Pike family, Esocidae (page 77)

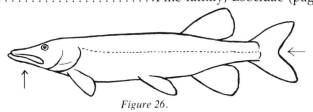

Figure 26.

17b. Jaws not duckbill-shaped, tail rounded .... go to 18
18a. Lower jaw protruding (Figure 27)
.... Killifish family, Cyprinodontidae (page 186)

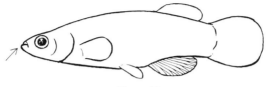

Figure 27.

18b. Lower jaw not protruding (Figure 28)
.... Mudminnow family, Umbridae (page 82)

Figure 28.

19a. Gill membranes attached under eye or in front of it
....go to 20
19b. Gill membranes attached distinctly behind eye
....go to 21
20a. Lateral line present (Figure 29)
.... Mooneye family, Hiodontidae (page 70)

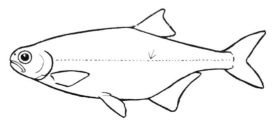

Figure 29.

20b. Lateral line absent (Figure 30)
........................Herring family, Clupeidae (page 72)

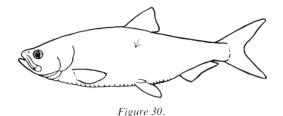

Figure 30.

21a. Dorsal fin with ten or more rays (Figure 31)
..............Sucker family, Catostomidae (page 150), and
two introduced minnows, carp (page 110)
and goldfish (page 111)

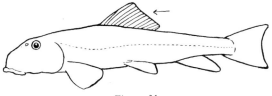

Figure 31.

21b. Dorsal fin with fewer than ten rays (Figure 32)
.... Minnow family, Cyprinidae (page 108)

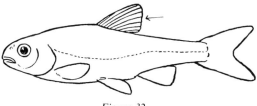

Figure 32.

22a. Vent in front of pectoral fins (Figure 33)
.........Pirate perch family, Aphredoderidae (page 183)

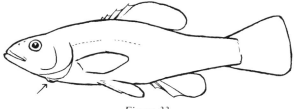

Figure 33.

22b. Vent behind pectoral fins .... go to 23
23a. Three or more spines in anal fin .... go to 24
23b. Two spines in anal fin .... go to 25
24a. Five or more longitudinal stripes (Figure 34)
.... Temperate bass family, Percichthyidae (page 197)

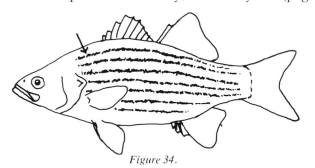

Figure 34.

24b. One longitudinal stripe or no longitudinal stripes (Figure 35) .... Sunfish family, Centrarchidae (page 200)

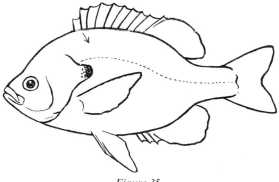

Figure 35.

25a. Lateral line extending through tail fin (Figure 36)
.... Drum family, Sciaenidae (page 239)

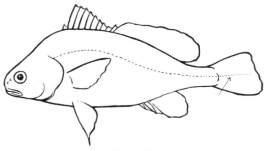

Figure 36.

25b. Lateral line not extending through tail fin (Figure 37)
.... Perch family, Percidae (page 216)

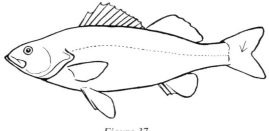

Figure 37.

Families of Minnesota Fishes

The 149 species of fishes in Minnesota today include 135 native species and 14 introduced species. The introduced species have been brought into the state either deliberately (for example, the coho salmon and the rainbow trout) or accidentally (for example, the sea lamprey and the alewife). The total of 149 is derived by excluding (1) species that have been introduced into Minnesota but have failed to establish themselves there (such as the Kokanee salmon, the cutthroat trout, the Ohrid trout, and the mosquitofish), (2) species known from the Mississippi River in northern Iowa but unverified in Minnesota (such as the black buffalo and the grass pickerel), and (3) one species that seems to be extinct in Minnesota (the skipjack). (Some authorities still include the mosquitofish, *Gambusia affinis,* in Minnesota's fauna. It was stocked extensively in the metropolitan area around the Twin Cities [Anoka, Hennepin, Ramsey, Scott, and Washington counties] in 1958, 1959, and 1960 in the hope that it would control mosquitoes by eating their aquatic larvae. The mosquitofish survived at least one winter in a few ponds, but it has not been seen in Minnesota since 1960 and presumably it is no longer extant in the state.)

Minnesota's fishes are classified into 26 families. Learning the common names of families helps one become familiar with Minnesota's fishes because these names tell what kinds are in each family (for example, the minnow family, the catfish family, and the sunfish family).

The accompanying chart lists the number of species represented from each family among Minnesota fishes. It shows the minnow family (Cyprinidae) in first place, with 44 species. (Although some people use the name minnow informally to mean any small fish, minnows do compose one distinct family. Most minnows are indeed small, but a few, such as the grass carp, are large fishes that can weigh as much as 100 pounds.) These 44 species of minnows compose almost one-third (30 percent) of the number of species of fishes in the state. Besides being diverse, Minnesota's minnows are abundant and provide a vital source of food for the more glamorous game fishes. Never underestimate the power of a minnow!

The perch family (Percidae) is in second place, with 18 species. All 18 are native and 3 of them (perch, sauger, and walleye) are familiar. The remaining 15 kinds are small fishes called darters that inhabit large and small streams. The most famous darter is the snail darter (not found in Minnesota), a rare fish whose endangered status gave it legal protection from the destruction of its habitat. The protection of the snail darter delayed the completion of the controversial Tellico Dam in Tennessee.

The salmon family (Salmonidae) is in third place, with 17 species. Only 10 of the salmonids are native to Minnesota, and

Number of Species in Families of Fishes as They Occur in Minnesota

Family	Number of Native Species in Minnesota	Number of Introduced Species in Minnesota (Includes Those Introduced Accidentally)	Total Number of Species in Family in Minnesota	Percentage of Species in Minnesota (Total of 149 Species)
1. Cyprinidae (minnows)	41	3	44	29.5
2. Percidae (perches)	18	0	18	12.1
3. Salmonidae (salmons, whitefishes)	10	7	17	11.4
4. Catostomidae (suckers)	16	0	16	10.7
5. Centrarchidae (sunfishes)	11	0	11	7.4
6. Ictaluridae (catfishes)	8	1	9	6.0
7. Petromyzontidae (lampreys)	3	1	4	2.7
8. Cottidae (sculpins)	4	0	4	2.7
9. Eight families each have two species in Minnesota	15	1 (alewife, family Clupeidae)	16	10.7
10. Ten families each have one species in Minnesota	9	1 (smelt, family Osmeridae)	10	6.7
TOTALS	135	14	149	100%

the other 7 are introduced. As the chart shows, other major families of fishes in Minnesota are the sucker family (Catostomidae) with 16 species, the sunfish family (Centrarchidae) with 11, and the catfish family (Ictaluridae) with 9. Of the remaining 20 families, 2 have 4 species in Minnesota, 8 have 2, and 10 have only 1.

Distribution of Minnesota Fishes

All of Minnesota but its southeastern and southwestern tips was buried beneath a vast sheet of ice, a glacier, until less than 10,000 years ago. Only with the northward retreat of the glacier did waterways for occupation and dispersal by fishes become available. Fishes swimming up the Mississippi could reach streams and lakes over much of Minnesota through waters created by glacial melting, and most of the kinds of fishes found in the state today probably are the descendants of fishes that did so. Some — such as the lake trout, the whitefishes, the lake chub, and the longnose sucker — range more to the north than to the south, and they probably occupied refuges relatively close to the glacier before its retreat.

St. Anthony Falls, in Minneapolis, has served as a barrier to fish migration from the Mississippi River south of the Twin Cities to the upper river since the retreat of the last glacier. Today, a lock and dam constructed more than a decade ago provides a route for the potential movement of species around the barrier falls, but to date no evidence has been found to support the existence of such movements of fishes.

As the glacier retreated, its meltwaters receded to a point where the major drainage areas became separated. Today, Minnesota's waters flow toward the sea in three widely divergent directions — North Shore streams to Lake Superior and ultimately to the Atlantic, Red River and Rainy River streams to Hudson Bay, and Mississippi streams to the Gulf of Mexico (Figure 38). A fish living in the headwaters of the Mississippi that wanted to get to the headwater streams of the Rainy River a few miles away would have a long trip: all the way down the Mississippi and across the Gulf of Mexico to the Atlantic, up the

Atlantic to Hudson Bay, and back through Canada to the Rainy
River system, a distance of more than 7,000 miles!

The glacier left a setting favorable to fishes. It carved many of

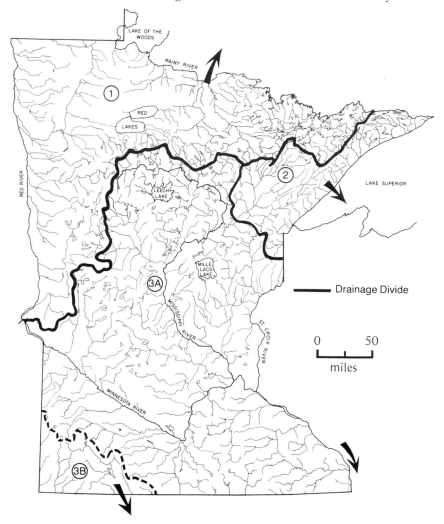

Figure 38. Major drainage systems of Minnesota: (1) Hudson Bay drainage
system, (2) Great Lakes drainage system, (3a) Mississippi River and
tributaries, (3b) Missouri River basin. The Missouri joins the Mississippi to
the south. Arrows denote general directions of flow.

the gorges and depressions for Minnesota's abundant lakes and streams in which fishes found their homes. The glacier left not only an abundance of habitat for fishes, but a diversity as well. Most kinds of fishes have preferred habitats, whether lakes, large rivers, or cold streams. Although Minnesota has fishes everywhere, the same kinds are not found everywhere and the types that are abundant vary from place to place. Fish habitats in Minnesota are so diverse that it is unrealistic to place them in just a few categories, and some fishes are much more versatile than others in the habitats that they can occupy. Even so, some general associations of certain species with certain habitats are recognizable.

Lake Habitats

Lake Superior. With its size and its depths of cold, clear water, Lake Superior is a habitat different from any inland Minnesota lake. Some fishes, such as the siscowet and five species of whitefishes (round whitefish, pygmy whitefish, shortjaw cisco, bloater, and kiyi), are known in Minnesota only from Lake Superior. The lake trout and the deepwater sculpin, although found in other habitats, are most abundant in Lake Superior.

Some Lake Superior fishes, such as the native longnose sucker and the introduced sea lamprey, pink salmon, coho salmon, chinook salmon, rainbow trout, brown trout, and rainbow smelt, all swim up North Shore streams to spawn. After spawning, the adults of the introduced species are exhausted and many soon die. The young that hatch remain in the streams for varying lengths of time depending on the life cycle of the species and go back to the lake to mature, thus beginning the cycle anew.

Lake Trout Lakes. Lakes of northern St. Louis, Lake, and Cook counties in northeastern Minnesota (Figure 39) are rocky and cold. The predominant game fish in these lakes is the lake trout. Other species common in these lakes include the northern pike, lake whitefish, tullibee, white sucker, and longnose sucker. The smallmouth bass, grayling, and splake (a hybrid of a male brook trout and a female lake trout) have all been introduced. A variety of minnows provides food for the larger fishes.

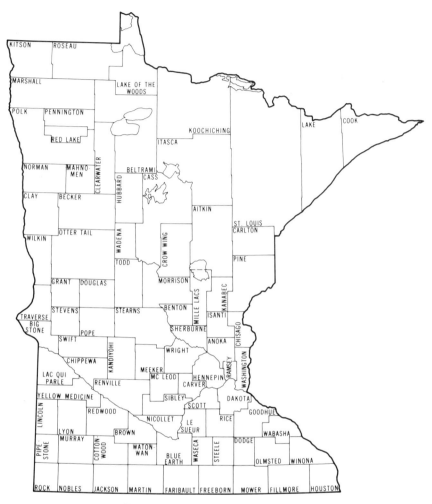

Figure 39. Counties of Minnesota.

Walleye Lakes. Various lakes in northern and central Minnesota are characterized by good walleye fishing. Lakes such as Mille Lacs, Leech, and the Red Lakes are nationally famous. Some of the best walleye lakes are broad and shallow and have winds that never seem to quit. Mille Lacs is a classic example. In these lakes, walleyes readily range over the sandy and rocky bottoms in well-oxygenated water. Other important fishes in these lakes include the northern pike, largemouth bass, yellow perch, tullibee, and burbot and the crappies, suckers, and minnows.

Bass–Panfish Lakes. Many lakes in central Minnesota are smaller, less open to wind, and more fertile than walleye lakes. In these lakes, the fishes caught most commonly are panfishes (sunfishes and crappies). Other important fishes in these lakes include the largemouth bass, northern pike, bullheads, yellow perch, and walleye.

Game Fish–Rough Fish Lakes. In south-central and southwestern Minnesota, lakes are typically warm, shallow, and rich in nutrients. The most abundant fishes there are those that can tolerate warm and cloudy water that is at times low in oxygen. The northern pike, largemouth bass, panfishes, and bullheads provide most of the sportfishing. Other abundant fishes in these lakes include suckers, the carp, and native minnows.

Stream Habitats

Rivers. Certain Minnesota fishes — such as the paddlefish, silver chub, bullhead minnow, blue sucker, spotted sucker, river redhorse, greater redhorse, channel catfish, flathead catfish, white bass, yellow bass, and crystal darter and the gars, buffalofishes, and carpsuckers — all occur naturally in large rivers far more often than in small streams or in lakes. A glance at this list explains why lakes are more interesting to many anglers — the most important game fishes are more abundant in lakes. Rivers do offer sportfishing for northern pike, saugers, and walleyes, and for catfishes and crappies. In fact, the walleye probably is primarily a natural river-dwelling fish in Minnesota, but extensive introductions of it into lakes have drastically changed its natural distribution.

Trout Streams. Minnesota has 481 designated trout streams, which ripple and splash over about 1,600 linear miles. Most of these streams are along the North Shore or in the southeastern part of the state. Some of them are among Minnesota's most intensively managed waters. The only native stream-dwelling trout in Minnesota is the brook trout. The rainbow trout and the brown trout have both been introduced. Trout populations, even of brook trout, are maintained in many streams through stocking. Other fishes typically found in trout streams are certain minnows, suckers, and sculpins.

Warm-Water Streams. The other small streams of Minnesota form a miscellaneous category most easily defined as those that do not support trout. Warm-water streams are important as "minnow streams" that produce small bait fishes. Minnesota's streams are varied and fascinating. For a lively and authoritative discussion of them, the reader should refer to *The Streams and Rivers of Minnesota* (Waters, 1977).

The most important game fishes in warm-water streams are the smallmouth bass and the panfishes. Small, relatively unfamiliar fishes, especially minnows and darters, thrive in many such streams. The shallow water of small, clear streams provides the opportunity for one to observe these small and numerous fishes at work and play. It is especially fun to watch minnows from the bank of a small stream when several kinds of them gather together over spawning beds in the spring. Certain minnows develop bright breeding colors at this time, and their building nests of pebbles, chasing, fighting, and spawning create a busy and colorful scene.

Introduced Fishes

Some of the most important Minnesota fishes have been introduced from elsewhere. Most of these introduced species are members of the salmon family that have been imported by the Minnesota Department of Natural Resources (DNR) to enhance sportfishing. The arctic grayling, coho salmon, chinook salmon, rainbow trout, and brown trout have all added to the richness of Minnesota fishing. The pink salmon reached Minnesota after having been accidentally introduced into the Great Lakes in Ontario. Another accidentally introduced fish that has added another dimension to fishing in Minnesota is the rainbow smelt, which escaped into the Great Lakes from lakes into which it had been introduced in Michigan. Tons of smelt are netted in the smelt run that takes place each spring along Lake Superior's North Shore.

The Minnesota fish fauna would be better off today if two of its immigrants, the sea lamprey and the carp, had stayed home. The sea lamprey is a primitive, predaceous fish that attacks and attaches itself to other fishes. A native of the Atlantic and Lake Ontario, it invaded the western Great Lakes via the Welland Canal near Niagara Falls and destroyed the lake trout (an important commercial fish) and other fishes in Lake Michigan and Lake Superior.

The carp is probably even more infamous than the sea lamprey because of its widespread occurrence. It seems strange now, but the carp was deliberately and intensively introduced from Europe in several places in this country, including Minnesota, in the last quarter of the nineteenth century. A desirable fish when cultured, the carp, once free, quickly turned into a prolifically breeding, adaptable fish. Declines in populations of native fishes have been noted where the carp is present. It is not pleasant to anticipate the possible invasion of another large and similar minnow, the grass carp, which has access to Minnesota through the Mississippi River system. (See the descriptions.)

Other introduced fishes — such as the goldfish, alewife, and mosquitofish — have had little impact in Minnesota. The recently introduced blue catfish may become an important sport fish in time. Some local populations of minnows have probably become established as a result of the discarding of unused bait fishes by anglers. Bait fishes should not be released, because they could become pests in new habitats.

How Big Do They Get?

When someone says "I caught a fish," one of the questions likely to be asked is "How big was it?" The large game fishes get the most attention, but Minnesota's fishes come in all sizes, from tiny to huge. The largest fish in Minnesota is the lake sturgeon, which occasionally exceeds 200 pounds. The smallest, the least darter, reaches a length of about 1½ inches, so its scientific name as printed here, *Etheostoma microperca,* is about as long as the fish itself.

The largest sturgeon from Minnesota on record is a 236-pound specimen taken in Lake of the Woods in 1911. Because it is not known for certain how this fish was caught, the state hook-and-line record appears to be a 162½-pounder caught in the Rainy River in 1968.

After the lake sturgeon, the fishes having the greatest growth potentials in Minnesota are probably the flathead catfish and the blue catfish. A 157-pound catfish, said to be a flathead, was supposedly taken in the Minnesota River on a set line (date unknown). The Minnesota hook-and-line record for the flathead is 70 pounds. The blue catfish, recently stocked in Minnesota, reaches a weight well over 100 pounds in the southern United States and could become one of the largest Minnesota fishes. The paddlefish, which grows to a weight of about 150 pounds in the south, is smaller in Minnesota, where it reaches about 50 pounds.

The Minnesota record for the muskellunge is 54 pounds. The state record for the northern pike, 45 pounds, 12 ounces, has stood for more than 50 years and is the oldest record in the Minnesota book. By contrast, shiny new records for the chinook salmon, pink salmon, rock bass, walleye, and other species have been set within the last 3 years.

The accompanying chart lists current record-size fishes caught by hook and line in Minnesota. Anyone who catches a fish believed to be a new state record should take the fish to a Minnesota DNR Section of Fisheries field station or to the DNR central office in the Centennial Building in St. Paul, have its weight verified on a state-certified retail scale in the presence of at least one witness, and fill in a Minnesota state record fish application form, which is to be notarized and submitted to the DNR with a clear, full-length photograph of the fish. The applicant must keep the fish for inspection until it is either accepted or rejected as a new record.

Anyone who catches a fish believed to be a world record should follow all of these procedures and apply to the International Game Fish Association in Fort Lauderdale, Florida, and to the National Fresh Water Fishing Hall of Fame in Hayward, Wisconsin, for a world record application form.

Minnesota Record Fish Caught by Angling
(Based on records of the Minnesota Department of Natural Resources;
listed alphabetically)

Species	Weight (Pounds-Ounces)	Where Caught	Angler	Date
1. Black crappie	5-0	Vermillion River, near Hastings, Dakota County	Tom Christenson, Red Wing	1940
2. Bluegill	2-13	Lake Alice, Hubbard County	Bob Parker, Bemidji	1948
3. Brook trout	6-2	Pine Mountain Lake, Cook County	Wes Smith, Grand Marais	20 May 1967
4. Brown trout	16-8	Grindstone Lake, Pine County	Carl Lovgren, St. Paul	29 May 1961
5. Carp	55-5	Clearwater Lake, Wright County	Frank J. Ledwein, Annandale	10 July 1952
6. Channel catfish	38-0	Mississippi River, Minneapolis, Hennepin County	Terrence Fussy, Minneapolis	16 February 1975
7. Chinook salmon	23-6¾	Lake Superior, near Hovland, Cook County	Jon Sanger, Grand Marais	7 July 1981
8. Coho salmon	10-6½	Lake Superior, near Baptism River, Lake County	Louis Rohde, Coon Rapids	7 November 1970
9. Flathead catfish	70-0	St. Croix River, near Marine, Washington County	John Lee Roberts, Garden City, Iowa	13 August 1970
10. Lake sturgeon	162-8	Rainy River, Koochiching County	Allan Knaeble, Big Falls	15 May 1968
11. Lake trout	43-8	Lake Superior, near Hovland, Cook County	G. H. Nelson	30 May 1955

12. Largemouth bass	10-2	Prairie Lake, Itasca County	Harold Lehn, Bemidji	28 June 1961
13. Muskellunge	54-0	Lake Winni- bigoshish, Itasca County	Art Lyons, Bena	28 August 1957
14. Northern pike	45-12	Basswood Lake, Lake County	J. Schanken	16 May 1929
15. Pink salmon	2-13	Baptism River, Lake County	Todd Blum, Ely	16 September 1981
16. Rainbow trout	17-6	Knife River, near Lake Superior, Lake County	Ottway R. Stuberud, Knife River	19 January 1974
17. Rock bass	1-15	Mille Lacs Lake, Mille Lacs County	Jason Junghans, Plymouth	19 August 1981
18. Sauger	6-2½	Mississippi River, below Alma Dam, Wabasha County	Marilyn Larson, Winona	July 1964
19. Smallmouth bass	8-0	West Battle Lake, Otter Tail County	John Creighton, Minneapolis	1948
20. Splake	9-6	Pierz Lake, Cook County	Gerald Quade, Duluth	23 May 1971
21. Walleye	17-8	Seagull River, near Lake Saganaga, Cook County	LeRoy Chiovitte, Hermantown	13 May 1979
22. Yellow perch	3-4	Lake Plantaganette, Hubbard County	Merle Johnson, Bemidji	1945

Photographing Fishes

Photographing fishes is like photographing any wild animal and can be done under water with natural light in selected sites of native habitat. Even in some of the clearest of Minnesota lakes,

This section was written by William D. Schmid, University of Minnesota, who provided most of the color photographs for this book.

Underwater photo of bluegill, water depth about 2 meters, Nikonos camera.

like Square Lake north of Stillwater and Christmas Lake at Excelsior, however, the turbidity is still high enough to add an apparent grain to the photographs and to reduce definition. Small fishes are difficult to photograph in their underwater habitat because they almost always move out of the plane of focus when the photographer swims toward them for close-up shots. Distant pictures of minnow-size fishes all look alike; that is, the distinguishing features of color and form are only apparent in close-up photographs. The use of aquariums and artificial lighting not only provides closer and sharper photographs, it also yields consistent composition and makes the photography far easier than it could ever be in lakes or streams.

In the color plates for this book, the background was kept simple to accentuate the forms of the fishes. Washed sand and

Underwater photo of male and female Iowa darters, water depth about 1 meter, Nikonos camera.

gravel were used as a substrate, and a blue wall behind the aquariums provided background color of the sky hue. A few pictures were taken on 35-millimeter film, but most were shot on 120 professional ektachrome (EPR 120, daylight) with a Mamiya RB67 single-lens reflex camera with a 90-millimeter Mamiya-Sekor lens. The larger format of 120 film carried more detail upon enlargement, and the leaf shutter of this camera allowed synchronization with electronic flash at high speed to eliminate ghost images from ambient light. The film was exposed at its normal ASA of 64 (F:8, 1/250 sec) with an automatic, thyristor-controlled, electronic flash. The electronic flash produced proper color balance on daylight film in addition to providing the high-speed exposure necessary to stop the action of swimming fishes. The camera was placed in position on a tripod, but the flash unit was held by hand and aimed downward to avoid direct flashback off the aquarium glass. The fishes were teased into position by gentle strokes with the handle of an aquarium net; then, the camera was quickly focused and the picture was taken. Of course, there were many times when the fishes moved just before the shutter was tripped. In some cases, the specimens would not stop swimming, so it was necessary to shoot at moving targets and hope for the best. About 300 exposures were made for the color plates in this book.

Fishes as Food

Fishing is an enjoyable, relaxing, surprising, and rewarding sport. Surprising in the sense of what you catch, a bullhead, burbot, or walleye, rewarding in that you get to cook and eat the surprise. As the late gourmet cook and learned fisheries biologist John Dobie wrote, "Here are some mouthwatering techniques for the intrepid kitchen connoisseur." The kitchen connoisseur must be careful not to overcook the fish; when the flesh "flakes" when scraped with a fork, it is done.

This section is adapted from "Cooking Your Catch," by John Dobie, an article that appeared in the May–June 1976 issue of *The Minnesota Volunteer*, a bimonthly magazine published by the Minnesota Department of Natural Resources. Used with permission of the publisher.

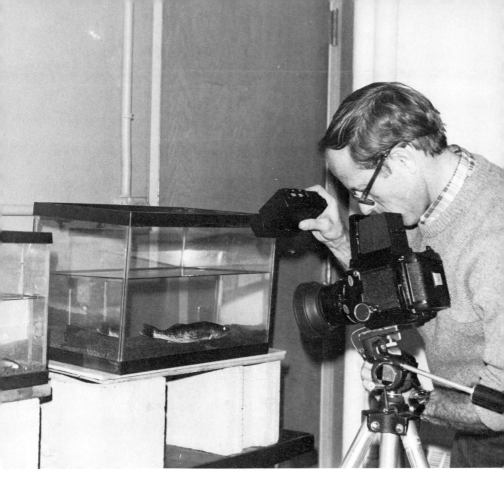

Setup for photographing fishes.

Fishes can be prepared for cooking in various ways. After the fish has been scaled and the head, fins, and entrails have been removed, the fish can be fried, baked, broiled, or poached. All types of fish scalers that have been manufactured, rivaling mouse traps in their variety, but again the common fork with the tines bent at a 90-degree angle to the handle works about as well as anything. Fish are most easily scaled when freshly caught and before the body surface has dried out.

Frying Panfish

Clean fish; wash and dry. Salt fish at least ½ hour before frying. Roll fish in peppered flour, and fry in salt pork drippings until brown. Turn fish; add ½ lemon sliced and 1 tablespoon of water. Cover and steam for 5 minutes. Turn again, add 1 table-spoon of butter, and fry until crisp on the outside.

Broiled Panfish

Sunfish and crappies are seldom broiled, but they are deli-cious prepared this way. Remove the scales, heads, and entrails from 12 freshly caught sunfish or crappies. Brush with cooking oil or melted butter and season with salt, pepper, and thyme or basil. Broil for 10 minutes. Turn and repeat this process. Serve with boiled potatoes.

Barbecued Sunfish

Marinate whole cleaned sunfish or crappies in a barbecue sauce for ½ hour. Serve hot off the grill.

Barbecue sauce. Beat 1 egg, add 1 cup of cooking oil, and beat again. Add ½ cup of vinegar, 1½ tablespoons of salt, 1 table-spoon of poultry seasoning, 1 teaspoon of pepper, and a pinch of garlic powder, and beat again.

Poached Bass

Bass sometimes have a muddy taste, but the following recipe will make bass taste as good as any other warm-water fish. Skin and fillet bass. Place on well-buttered ovenproof dish. Pour on ½ cup of dry sherry, cover, and poach in a moderate oven for 25 minutes. Remove and place fish on platter. Keep hot until needed. Melt 3 tablespoons of butter in sauce pan, season, and stir in 2 tablespoons of flour. Pour in strained liquid from bass and thicken over fire. Add ¾ cup of milk and bring to boil. Pour sauce over fish.

Fish Patties

Youngsters love to fish, and the measure of success is not size but numbers. They treasure their catch, and often you come home with many small fish, fish too small to cook in the usual manner. Quite often these small fish are discarded, but they can be used by making them into patties. Sunfish make delicious patties.

Remove scales, heads, fins, entrails, and backbone. Grind the fish through the fine blade of a food grinder. Several grindings may be necessary to reduce the rib bones to a size that will not be noticed when the fish is cooked. Add one egg, salt, and pepper to the ground fish. Mix thoroughly and form into patties. The patties can be rolled in either flour or bread crumbs and fried in melted butter until brown. This tasty technique can be used for burbot, perch, and northern pike. Excess patties may be wrapped in foil and frozen for future use.

Broiled Walleye or Perch

Fillet the fish and remove the skin. Next, wash and dry the fillets and place on a broiled rack. Baste with melted butter, season with salt and pepper, and broil for 7 to 10 minutes, depending on the closeness of the heat source. Turn the fillets, and repeat the process. The flavor of walleye and perch is so good that condiments are unnecessary.

Walleye Fillets in Lemon Butter

When John Dobie was in Italy attending an international limnology meeting, he discovered this recipe. In Italy it was used with sole. Cut up enough walleyes so each guest can have a good-sized fillet or two small pieces. Wash the fillets in cold water and dry thoroughly.

Cover the bottom of an ovenproof casserole with melted butter. Mix in tablespoon of lemon juice. Season the fillets with salt and freshly ground pepper, and place in casserole in a single layer. Cover the casserole and bake at 350° Fahrenheit (F) until the fish flakes easily. Remove to a hot platter, and serve with boiled potatoes and a green vegetable.

Baked Northern Pike

Wash and dry 2 pounds of northern pike fillets. Dip fish in ½ cup of milk seasoned with 2 tablespoons of salt. Roll in 1½ cups of slightly crushed corn flakes. Melt 2 tablespoons of butter and pour over fish. Bake in an oven at 400° F for 20 minutes. Serve with tartar sauce.

Broiled Northern Pike

Brush northern pike fillets with soy sauce and allow to stand for 10 to 15 minutes. Brush fillets with melted butter and broil until lightly brown. Turn, brush with butter again, and broil until tender. Serve with lemon wedges.

Fried Burbot

Many burbot, or eelpout, are caught by winter fishermen and tossed on the ice to die. This is certainly a waste of tasty fish. Burbot ranks close to walleye in eating quality, and to a few gourmets it is considered superior. Burbot has firm, white flesh that flakes with the touch of a fork. It has a slightly codfish taste.

Skin the fish, and remove the tenderloin, the portion along the backbone. Wash in cold water. Cut the tenderloin into scallop-sized pieces, season with salt and pepper, roll in beaten egg, and dredge in flour or bread crumbs. Fry in butter or hot oil until well browned.

Baked Fish

Any large fish, whether lake trout, salmon, catfish, northern pike, muskellunge, carp, or buffalo, can be baked for a delicious meal. Baking is a good method for cooking oily fish or those with soft flesh, because the skin and binding will hold the fish in shape while it is cooking.

Most fish are baked whole, and so they should be prepared to look good on the serving platter. Carp and buffalo should be fleeced, that is, the scales and outer skin should be removed while leaving the inner skin to hold the fish intact during cooking. Trout and salmon need only be gutted and cleaned. Their scales are so small they do not have to be removed.

After the fish is washed and dried, season it inside and out with salt and pepper. Place stuffing in the cavity, and bind the fish with string, or fasten it together with skewers. Cover the fish with strips of bacon held in place with toothpicks, and place in a roaster or casserole. Place ½ cup of chicken broth, several sliced onions, 1 sliced carrot, and 2 tablespoons of dry sherry wine in the roaster or casserole. Cover the fish, and cook in a moderate oven until tender.

Bread Stuffing and Topping for Baked Fish

Melt ½ cup of butter and add ½ cup of finely chopped onion, ½ cup of chopped celery, 2 teaspoons of salt, ¼ teaspoon of coarse ground pepper, and 1 teaspoon of chervil. Saute the vegetables for 5 minutes. Add 4 cups of bread cubes and toss lightly until the butter has been absorbed by the bread. Pour the bread cubes and vegetables into a large bowl, mix together, and add enough hot water to moisten the bread cubes slightly. Press a small amount of stuffing between your fingers. If stuffing does not stick together, add more hot water.

You may not care for bacon flavor; if not, omit bacon strips and instead baste the fish periodically with cooking oil to prevent drying. Just before serving, the top side of the fish can be sprinkled with bread crumbs moistened with wine and placed under the broiler until the crumbs are brown.

Marinated Trout

This recipe is good for a large rainbow, brown, or lake trout. Soak trout fillets or steaks in a marinade of wine, salt, pepper, basil, and garlic powder for ½ hour. Roll in soft bread crumbs, then in beaten eggs, and again in soft bread crumbs. Broil 10 minutes, basting several times with wine sauce. Turn and broil for another 10 minutes, basting several more times. Place fillets on a warm platter and cover with melted butter seasoned with finely chopped parsley.

Trout Amandine

Sprinkle 6 cleaned trout with salt, coarse ground pepper, and thyme. Dip in milk and then in flour. Lay trout in shallow hot peanut oil in a skillet; fry to a golden brown on both sides. Drain off oil. Add ¼ cup of butter and ½ cup of slivered almonds; cook until the almonds are brown. Remove trout to a heated platter, top with butter and almonds, and sprinkle with chopped parsley.

Whitefish, Tullibee, and Herring

These delightful and delicious fish are rarely taken by hook-and-line fishing. However, they can be caught at certain times of the year by the angler. More often they are taken in gill nets during the special fall season. They are usually pan fried, smoked, or pickled, but they may also be cooked in other ways.

Baked Whitefish

Scale a 2- or 3-pound whitefish or tullibee; remove head, fins, and entrails. Season inside and out with salt and pepper. Stuff cavity with whole mushrooms that have been washed, dried, and seasoned with salt and pepper. Place fish in a pan or oven-proof casserole, and add any surplus mushrooms. Brush fish and mushrooms with melted butter and cover with sour cream. Pour 2 or 3 tablespoons of dry white wine into the pan. Bake fish for 45 to 60 minutes. Remove to a hot platter and serve with boiled potatoes. John's Scandinavian friends suggested that the fish be seasoned with dill.

Fried Catfish and Bullheads

These popular fish are usually cleaned, washed, dried, dipped in lightly beaten egg, rolled in flour, and either pan fried or deep fried until crisp on the outside. They are usually served with hush puppies or boiled potatoes.

Hush Puppies. Add 2 cups of cornmeal and 2 tablespoons of flour to 3½ cups of boiling water, mix well, and let cool. Add 1½ teaspoons of salt, 1 teaspoon of baking powder, 2 tablespoons of melted butter, 2 tablespoons of grated onion, and ½ teaspoon of black pepper. Mix well. For each hush puppy drop 1 teaspoon of this mixture on a hot, well-greased griddle.

Sauces to Serve with Fish

Many people feel that cooked fish has a rather bland flavor, so a sauce is often necessary. Following are some popular sauces for fish.

Tartar Sauce. Mix together 1 teaspoon each of finely chopped parsley, shallot, sweet gherkins, and olives. Add 1 teaspoon of prepared mustard, salt and freshly ground pepper to taste, and 1 cup of mayonnaise.

Hollandaise Sauce. Cut ¼ pound of butter into 3 pieces. Melt 1 piece of butter with 3 egg yolks by stirring together in a saucepan held in a pan of hot water (not boiling). When the first piece has blended thoroughly, add the second piece of butter and stir until blended. Then add the third piece and stir. Remove from hot water and stir for 2 minutes. Add 2 teaspoons of lemon juice and salt and white pepper to taste. Return saucepan to hot water and stir for 2 minutes more.

Polonaise Sauce. Heat 6 tablespoons of butter and, when it begins to brown slightly, add 3 tablespoons of fine bread crumbs. Cook until the crumbs are brown and the butter has stopped bubbling. Add a few drops of lemon juice and finely chopped parsley to taste.

Storing Fish

If you are so fortunate as to catch more fish than can be eaten at once, freeze them. Clean your catch; remove fins, heads, and entrails; scale or fillet as you choose. Do not wash the fish or fillets; simply damp dry them with paper toweling. They will keep much longer, and you will avoid that strong "fishy taste" that many people object to in fish. Once a fish is cleaned, it can be stored in several ways. Small fish can be allowed to freeze in a block of ice. Fillets and whole fish can be wrapped in several layers of heavy aluminum foil or plastic wrap. Be certain that the fish are wrapped carefully to avoid the strong flavors that develop when the fish dry out. Fillets and whole fish can also be frozen in the freezer and then dipped in ice water to produce an ice glaze. The process is repeated several times.

Small stream trout can be frozen separately and then wrapped in aluminum foil packages in meal-size portions. Store frozen fish in the coldest part of the freezer. A temperature of −10° F is best. Extension nutritionists at the University of Minnesota (Verna Mikesh and Grace Brill. 1968. *Fresh Water Fish — Care and Cooking.* University of Minnesota, Agricultural Extension Service, Bulletin 356, 14 pp.) give the following storage life for fish frozen at 0° F or lower. Northern pike, lake trout, smelt — 4 to 6 months. Bluegills, bass, crappies, sunfish — 7 to 9 months. Walleyes and perch — 9 months or more.

Habitat Changes

The human impact on the waters of Minnesota is so profound that it seems safe to say that the distribution and abundance of every kind of fish in the state have been affected by it to some degree. Agricultural practices that lead to erosion and subsequent siltation of streams, drainage of lowlands, industrial and domestic pollution, generation of acid rain that can increase the acidity of lake water, construction of dams, and development of waterfront property are all putting an ever-increasing strain on fish populations. The uses that people make of water contribute to the two basic conditions that cause fish populations to decrease — degraded water quality and disappearance of habitat.

All fishes are adversely affected by the decreasing quality of habitat, some more than others. Evidence suggests clearly that such fishes as the American brook lamprey, lake sturgeon, paddlefish, blue sucker, stonecat, and walleye and certain redhorses and minnows have all declined in their river and stream habitats in Minnesota because of pollution and turbidity. Ditching and draining lowlands have apparently caused such fishes as the bigmouth buffalo, the northern pike (which spawns in sloughs), the hog sucker, and the pirate perch to suffer loss of habitat in some places.

In the past 20 years, some Minnesota lakes have turned from clear and blue to cloudy and green, with an accompanying decline in their beauty and in the quality of water sports. The main cause of this change is nutrient pollution, the introduction of nutritional substances for plant growth into water, chiefly through domestic sources such as human wastes and detergents and agricultural sources such as natural and artificial fertilizers. Nutrients from all sources do, in fact, act as fertilizers, stimulating plants to grow in water just as they do on land. Rooted aquatic plants and algae capture the sun's energy by photosynthesis and grow by using the nutrients in the water. If excessive nutrients are present, plant growth can be explosive. Lakes characterized by abundant nutrients and plant growth are said to be enriched , or **eutrophic.** The changes that occur in a lake as it becomes eutrophic are complex, but in the process rough fishes (such as carp and bullheads) tend to replace large game fishes. It is true that some desirable fishes thrive in eutrophic lakes; but for some of them, such as sunfishes, the results of the loss of nature's balance often manifest themselves in the form of populations of stunted fishes whose numbers are not controlled by predators.

Dams have altered the habitats of fishes by turning flowing water into lake impoundments. In other states, fishes such as the paddlefish, silver bass, yellow bass, and sauger and the catfishes have done well in impoundments and make for good fishing. The native fauna, however, is lost forever. An interesting and seemingly unanticipated effect of dams on fishes is the blocking of fish migrations. The migrations of the American eel up the Mississippi to Minnesota have declined, probably because of pollution and large dams. The spawning migration of the shovelnose sturgeon into the upper reaches of the St. Croix is blocked by a dam at Taylors Falls. Dams have apparently contributed directly to the loss of the skipjack from the Minnesota fish fauna within this century. The skipjack is a migratory fish that uses the Mississippi as its main avenue of travel. It was taken in Minnesota in the Mississippi, the St. Croix, and, as late as 1920, even in Big Stone Lake near the headwaters of the Minnesota River. Dams, probably the dam completed in 1913 near Keokuk, Iowa, primarily, have apparently eliminated the skipjack from the upper Mississippi region. The loss of even this seemingly unimportant fish offers a lesson in ecology, for the skipjack is the only fish known to carry larvae of the species of clam that was of primary importance to the button-making industry in Minnesota. With the loss of the skipjack and with the concurrent pollution of the river came the loss of jobs associated with the presence of the pearl-button industry's most valuable clam.

Serious concern has developed recently in Minnesota regarding acid rain, rainfall that carries acids that have formed in the atmosphere from the chemical interaction between water and airborne wastes produced by industrial and transportational combustion. Fish life in some lakes and streams in Norway, Sweden, and the eastern United States has already been destroyed by the effects of acid rain, which can make water too acidic to allow the sensitive eggs and young of fishes or certain organisms vital to the **food chain** to survive. The precious lake trout lakes of northeastern Minnesota, whose acidity is relatively easy to change because they are low in dissolved substances such as limestone that neutralize acids, are especially vulnerable to the menace of acid rain.

The St. Croix River offers a positive example of what good habitat means to fishes and people. With its scenery and clean water, the St. Croix is a popular recreational area that enjoys protection under the National Wild and Scenic Rivers Act of 1968. Some Minnesota fishes that inhabit rivers are more common in the St. Croix than in the other rivers to which they have access. Examples include the lake sturgeon, paddlefish, blue sucker, river redhorse, spotted sucker, walleye, and gilt darter. Redhorses seem to be quite sensitive to pollution and silt. The river redhorse is locally common in Lake St. Croix, the large river lake on the St. Croix. This redhorse is rare in the Mississippi River south of Minnesota. It was taken in the Minnesota River in the 1890s, but it has not been seen there recently. The implication is that its habitat has shrunk as the rivers in which it lives have become dirtier. Clean water is essential if the fish fauna of the Minnesota region is to retain its diversity and abundance.

Conservation of Fishes

The Minnesota DNR estimates that anglers spend more than $500 million in Minnesota every year, an amount that certainly has significant impact on the state's economy. The argument for the conservation of the fish resource rests on a solid economic foundation.

Little information on the fishes of Minnesota was available until late in the nineteenth century. The state's program for the propagation and distribution of fishes and the enforcement of fishing laws began in 1874 with the establishment of a Commission of Fisheries, the forerunner of the present Division of Fish and Wildlife of the DNR. In the 1890s, Prof. Ulysses O. Cox of the State Normal School at Mankato (today, Mankato State University) collected fishes from several places in the state and described them in two summary reports, the first on the fishes of southwestern Minnesota (1896) and the second on the fishes of the whole state (1897). Thaddeus Surber, the first biologist employed by the Game and Fish Commission, conducted surveys of Minnesota streams in the 1920s.

In 1931, the Minnesota state legislature established the five-member Conservation Commission that was reorganized in 1937 into the state Department of Conservation. Research on fishes within the department was given impetus by a series of lake surveys conducted between 1935 and 1940 under the direction of Prof. Samuel Eddy of the University of Minnesota. These lake surveys — in which studies of fishes, water chemistry, aquatic plants, and contour mapping were coordinated for the first time in Minnesota — established the basic methods by which surveys of the state's lakes and streams have been done ever since.

By legislative decree, the name of Minnesota's Department of Conservation was changed to the Department of Natural Resources as of Monday, January 4, 1971. It is with the Section of Fisheries of the DNR's Division of Fish and Wildlife that most of the burden of conserving Minnesota's fishes rests today. The manifold activities of the Section of Fisheries attest to the complexity of the task: fisheries personnel maintain hatcheries and rearing ponds, stock game fishes, trap and remove rough fishes, rehabilitate lakes, construct spawning areas for northern pike and other fishes, survey lakes and streams, improve habitats, and conduct basic research. Most of the funds on which the Section of Fisheries operates come from the purchase of licenses by anglers, who pay directly for the assurance that their sport will be there in the future.

In 1973, the United States Congress established the Endangered Species Act, which was designed to bring protection to endangered and threatened species of plants and animals. It defined an endangered species as one "in danger of extinction throughout all or a significant portion of its range" and a threatened species as one "likely to become an endangered species within the foreseeable future." No Minnesota fishes are on the federal list of endangered or threatened species. The Minnesota DNR also maintains a list of endangered and threatened species, this one with special reference to the state. Again, no fishes are considered endangered or threatened, but certain species are included in special categories. The paddlefish, lake sturgeon, and black redhorse are rated as species of changing or uncertain status, that is, ones that are uncommon or local in occurrence that could become threatened. The American brook lamprey, pugnose shiner, blue sucker, and least darter are rated as species of special interest, that is, ones that merit special consideration and should be watched to see that they do not become threatened. The blue catfish and the skipjack are considered to be extirpated or rare in Minnesota and to have little future there. The recent introduction of blue catfish could remove the species from this status.

While including the paddlefish, pugnose shiner, blue sucker, black redhorse, blue catfish, and least darter in lists of special categories, the DNR notes that these species have probably always been rare or uncommon in Minnesota and that some of them are probably at the periphery of their natural range there. It is possible that species that reach the limits of their natural range in Minnesota are less abundant there than elsewhere simply because they are near the limits of the environmental conditions that they need. Seventeen species of fishes living in the Mississippi or adjoining streams are confined in Minnesota to the southeastern sector even though the routes for northward dispersal are available. Pollution might inhibit the migration of some of these fishes today, but it seems likely that natural factors — possibly, for example, temperature — limit the range and abundance of certain fishes quite apart from the influence of human activities.

References

Systematics and Fish Distribution: Regional

Bailey, R. M., and M. O. Allum. 1962. *The Fishes of South Dakota*. Miscellaneous publication 119. Ann Arbor: University of Michigan, Museum of Zoology.

Becker, G. C. 1966. Fishes of southwestern Wisconsin. *Transactions of the Wisconsin Academy of Sciences, Arts, and Letters* 55:87–117.

Clay, W. M. 1975. *The Fishes of Kentucky*. Frankfort: Kentucky Department of Fish and Wildlife Resources.

Cross, F. B. 1967. *Handbook of Fishes of Kansas*. Miscellaneous publication 45. Lawrence: University of Kansas Museum of Natural History.

Forbes, S. E., and R. E. Richardson. 1920. *The Fishes of Illinois*. 2nd ed. Springfield: Natural History Survey of Illinois.

Greene, C. W. 1935. *The Distribution of Wisconsin Fishes*. Madison: Wisconsin Conservation Commission.

Harlan, J. R., and E. B. Speaker. 1969. *Iowa Fish and Fishing*. 4th ed. Des Moines: Iowa Conservation Commission.

Hubbs, C. L., and K. F. Lagler. 1964. *Fishes of the Great Lakes Region*. Ann Arbor: University of Michigan Press.

McPhail, J. D., and C. C. Lindsey. 1970. *Freshwater Fishes of Northwestern Canada and Alaska*. Bulletin 1973. Ottawa: Fisheries Research Board of Canada.

Miller, R. J., and H. W. Robison. 1973. *The Fishes of Oklahoma*. Stillwater: Oklahoma State University Press.

Moyle, P. B. 1976. *Inland Fishes of California*. Berkeley: University of California Press.

Pflieger, W. L. 1975. *The Fishes of Missouri*. Jefferson City: Missouri Department of Conservation.

Scott, W. B., and E. J. Crossman. 1973. *Freshwater Fishes of Canada*. Bulletin 184. Ottawa: Fisheries Research Board of Canada.

Smith, P. W. 1979. *The Fishes of Illinois*. Urbana: University of Illinois Press.

Trautman, M. B. 1957. *The Fishes of Ohio*. Columbus: Ohio State University Press.

Systematics and Fish Distribution: Minnesota

Cox, U. O. 1896. A report upon the fishes of southwestern Minnesota. *Report of the United States Fish Commission* (1894):605–16.

———. 1897. *A Preliminary Report on the Fishes of Minnesota*. Zoological series III. St. Paul: Geological and Natural History Survey of Minnesota.

Eddy, S., R. C. Tasker, and J. C. Underhill. 1972. *Fishes of the Red River, Rainy River, and Lake of the Woods, Minnesota, with*

Comments on the Distribution of Species in the Nelson River Drainage. Occasional paper 11. Minneapolis: University of Minnesota, Bell Museum of Natural History.

Eddy, S., and J. C. Underhill. 1974. *Northern Fishes*. 3rd ed. Minneapolis: University of Minnesota Press.

Evermann, B. W., and H. B. Latimer. 1910. The fishes of the Lake of the Woods and connecting waters. *Proceedings of the United States National Museum* 39:121–36.

Phillips, G. L., and J. C. Underhill. 1971. *Distribution and Variation of the Catostomidae of Minnesota*. Occasional paper 10. Minneapolis: University of Minnesota, Bell Museum of Natural History.

Underhill, J. C. 1957. *The Distribution of Minnesota Minnows and Darters in Relation to Pleistocene Glaciation*. Occasional paper 7. Minneapolis: University of Minnesota, Bell Museum of Natural History.

Underhill, J. C., and J. B. Moyle. 1968. The fishes of Minnesota's Lake Superior region. *Conservation Volunteer* 31:29–53.

Identification and Nomenclature

Eddy, S., and J. C. Underhill. 1978. *How to Know the Freshwater Fishes*. 3rd ed. Dubuque, Iowa: Wm. C. Brown.

Robins, C. R., R. M. Bailey, C. E. Bond, J. R. Brooker, E. A. Lachner, R. N. Lea, and W. B. Scott. 1980. *A List of Common and Scientific Names of Fishes from the United States and Canada*. 4th ed. Special publication 12. Bethesda, Md.: American Fisheries Society.

Sportfishing

(So many excellent books on sportfishing are available that it was necessary to limit the following list to those of special interest to Minnesota's anglers.)

Bates, J. D., Jr. 1973. *Fishing*. New York: E. P. Dutton.

Bergh, K. 1977. *Northern Pike Fishing*. Minneapolis: Dillon.

Fellegy, J., Jr. 1973. *Walleyes and Walleye Fishing*. Minneapolis: Dillon.

Haugstad, M. C. 1969. *Guidelines for Trout Fishing in Eastern-Central Minnesota*. St. Paul: Minnesota Department of Conservation.

Holland, D. 1979. *The Trout Fisherman's Bible*. Rev. ed. Garden City, N.Y.: Doubleday.

McNally, T. 1970. *Fisherman's Bible*. Chicago: Follette.

Meyers, C., and A. Lindner. 1978. *Catching Fish*. Minneapolis: Dillon.

Ovington, R. 1976. *Freshwater Fishing*. New York: Hawthorn Books.

Schara, R. 1977. *Muskie Mania*. Chicago: Contemporary Books.

———. 1978. *Minnesota Fishing Guide*. Minneapolis: Waldman House.

Snook, P. K. 1976. *The Compleat Guide to Fishing the Great Lakes*. Matteson, Illinois: Greatlakes Living Press.

Zumbro, J. 1978. *Icefishing East and West*. New York: David McKay.

Others

Breining, G., and L. Watson. 1977. *A Gathering of Waters: A Guide to Minnesota's Rivers*. St. Paul: Minnesota Department of Natural Resources.

Carlander, H. B. 1954. *A History of Fish and Fishing in the Upper Mississippi River*. Upper Mississippi River Conservation Committee.

Lawrie, A. H., and J. F. Fahrer. 1973. *Lake Superior, A Case History of the Lake and Its Fisheries*. Technical report 19. Ann Arbor: Great Lakes Fisheries Commission.

Mikesh, V., and G. Brill. 1968. *Fresh Water Fish — Care and Cooking*. Extension bulletin 356. St. Paul: University of Minnesota, Agricultural Extension Service.

Morris, D., and I. Morris. 1972. *The Complete Fish Cookbook*. South Hackensack, N.J.: Stoeger.

Moyle, J. B. 1975. . . . *The Uncommon Ones*. St. Paul: Minnesota Department of Natural Resources.

Ommaney, F. D. 1970. *The Fishes*. New York: Time-Life Books.

Schwartz, G. M., and G. A. Thiel. 1963. *Minnesota's Rocks and Waters*. Minneapolis: University of Minnesota Press.

Waters, T. F. 1977. *The Streams and Rivers of Minnesota*. Minneapolis: University of Minnesota Press.

Zim, H. S., and H. H. Shoemaker. 1956. *Fishes*. New York: Simon and Schuster.

Glossary

Abdominal. Referring to the lower surface of the body, especially the portion between the pectoral fins and the vent.
Adipose fin. A fleshy fin on the back behind the dorsal fin, as in catfishes.
Alevin. A newly hatched fish, usually a salmonid, still living off stored yolk.
Ammocoetes. A larval lamprey.
Anadromous. Swimming up rivers from the sea to spawn, as some salmons do.
Anal fin. The unpaired fin on the lower surface of the body behind the vent.

Barbels. Threadlike sensory structures on the head, as in catfishes.

Catadromous. Swimming down rivers to the sea to spawn, as the American eel does.
Caudal peduncle. The body trunk between the anal fin and the tail fin.

Dorsal fin. The unpaired fin on the upper surface of the body.

Eutrophic. Referring to a lake enriched by nutrients, with resulting heavy growth of aquatic plants.

Fingerling. A young fish, usually one late in its first year of life.
Food chain. The flow of food and energy from photosynthetic plants through a given series of consumers.
Fry. A young fish shortly after it has used its yolk and has started feeding actively.

Gill membrane. A membrane associated with the operculum that closes the gill cavity below it.
Gill rakers. Projections on bony arches in the gill region that serve in some fishes, such as the paddlefish, to trap small food organisms filtered from the water.

Hard (spinous) ray. A hardened fin ray, like that found in catfishes, that often has a series of toothlike points along one edge.
Heterocercal. Unequally lobed, as is the tail fin of sturgeons.

Homocercal. Equally lobed, as is the tail fin of most Minnesota fishes.

Jugular. Of the throat; referring to pelvic fins that are attached in front of the pectoral fins, as in the burbot.

Landlocked. Cut off from the sea and confined to fresh water by geographical barriers.

Larval. Referring to a larva, a young animal that differs greatly from the adult.

Lateral line. A series of porelike sensory openings along the side of a fish.

Oligotrophic. Referring to a lake that is low in nutrients, with relatively little growth of aquatic plants.

Operculum. The covering of the gills.

Pectoral fins. The forward or upper paired fins usually located above the pelvic fins.

Pelvic axillary process. A small projection near the base of each pelvic fin, as in the salmons.

Pelvic fins. The rearward or lower paired fins usually located below the pectoral fins.

Peritoneum. The membranous lining of the body cavity.

Pharyngeal teeth. Bony toothlike projections or plates associated with bones of the pharynx (throat region).

Plankton. Small floating plants and animals that serve as food for many fishes.

Soft rays. Flexible, jointed, branched structures that support a fin membrane.

Spines. Sharp, unjointed, unbranched structures in fins or pointed structures on other parts of the body, as the operculum, fin spines are usually stiff, as in the sunfishes, but can be flexible, as in the trout-perch.

Standard length. The distance from the tip of the snout to the structural base of the tail fin.

Subterminal. Referring to the position of a mouth that is at the front of the head but under, rather than at the tip of, the snout, as in most suckers.

Swim bladder. A gas-containing sac near the top of the body cavity.

Tail (caudal) fin. The unpaired fin that terminates the tail portion of the body.

Terminal. At the end; for example, a terminal mouth is at the front tip of the head.

Thoracic. Referring to the chest region.

Tubercles. Small, hardened, pointed or blunt projections from the skin. They are typically best developed in fishes at breeding time.

Vent. The opening of the digestive tract through which food wastes leave the body.

Ventral. On the lower surface.

Fishes of the Minnesota Region
Descriptions and Portraits

Family PETROMYZONTIDAE
The Lampreys

The lampreys are jawless fishes placed in the class Cyclostomata (*cyclo*, circular; *stomata*, mouth). They are referred to as round mouth eels because of their circular mouths and eellike bodies. Although lampreys resemble eels in shape (and are sometimes called lamprey eels), they are quite different from eels. The lampreys and their relatives, the marine hagfishes, in fact, represent the most primitive vertebrates (animals with backbones, or vertebrae) living today. The first lampreys appear in strata of Pennsylvanian age, 250 million years ago. Present-day lampreys differ little from their fossil ancestors.

The cyclostomes were descendants of the Ostracodermi (*osteo*, bone; *dermi*, skin), bony-skinned, jawless vertebrates that first appeared in Cambrian time, 500 million years ago. The remains of the ostracoderms constitute the earliest record of vertebrates in the fossil record. These early jawless fishes had bony armor to protect them from the large predaceous arthropods in the Paleozoic seas. The ostracoderms were filter feeders, and they strained organic matter from the water in a manner similar to the one used by the larvae of their modern descendants, the lampreys.

Ostracoderms disappeared from the geologic record during the latter part of the Devonian age, about 330 million years ago, and were replaced by the jawed fishes. The jawed fishes included the Placodermi (*placo*, plate; *dermi*, skin); the Chondrichthyes (*chondro*, cartilage; *ichthys*, fish), fishes with cartilaginous skeletons, the sharks, skates, and rays; and the Osteichthyes (*osteo*, bone; *ichthys*, fish), the bony fishes. The predaceous lampreys are the only remnant of the once important and diverse group of jawless fishes, the first vertebrates and the first fishes to dominate the ancient seas.

Sea Lamprey, *Petromyzon marinus* Linnaeus

Scientific name: *Petromyzon* = stone to suck (Greek); *marinus* = marine.

The sea lamprey, a marine species, first appeared in the Great Lakes a century after the construction of the Welland Canal in 1829. In 1946, the first specimens of sea lampreys were collected from Lake Superior. Shortly thereafter, the populations of lake trout and lake whitefish in the lake declined markedly.

The sea lamprey is one of a number of **anadromous** fishes (that is, species that live in lakes or oceans and make annual or periodic migrations into tributary streams to spawn) known from our lakes. The ancestors of the **landlocked** marine lampreys lived in the Atlantic Ocean and in the spring migrated up the major freshwater streams in eastern North America to spawn. Their descendants have adapted to living their entire lives in fresh water without the need to return as adults to the sea. The spawning lampreys construct a dish-shaped nest in a gravel riffle. The female is able to pick up stones by means of her circular mouth and move them from the nest site; this ability gives the generic name *Petromyzon* to the group. The female lays her eggs, up to 95,000 of them, and they are fertilized by the male. When the spawning act is completed, the adults die. The eggs hatch in about 20 days, and the larval lampreys (called **ammocoetes**) drift downstream from the nest site, settle to the bottom in a quiet eddy, and begin a 6- to 7-year, free-living, filter-feeding existence. Organic material is filtered from the water and trapped in mucous secretions, and the mucous threads plus organic material are swallowed. After about 7 years, the ammocoetes undergo a radical metamorphosis (a change into the predaceous adult form) and migrate back to the lake or the ocean. There they feed on various species of fishes by rasping holes in the sides of the fishes and digesting the cells and tissues of their prey. Young lampreys feed more frequently and for longer periods of time than do old individuals. The aftermath of the attack is usually death for the prey, either directly from the loss of fluids and tissues or indirectly from the secondary infection of the wound. Some fishes do survive (scarred lake trout appear occasionally), but these survivors are usually in very poor condition. In about a year, the lampreys mature and the following spring migrate upstream to spawn and die.

The weak link in the life cycle of the lamprey is the ammocoetes. The larvae are restricted to streams and are less dispersed than the adults in the lake, and the larval stage lasts six to seven years. Selective poisons called larvicides because they kill the ammocoetes but do not harm other aquatic organisms or terrestrial animals that might use the stream habitat have been developed. The sea lamprey has no known natural enemies in the Great Lakes, so the hope of fishery biologists is that, through control of the number of ammocoetes in the principal streams, the present stocks of salmons, trouts, and whitefishes may be maintained at a level to support a successful sport fishery. The biologists have been successful and the deep-sea fisheries in Lake Michigan and Lake Superior are once again exciting and productive.

The sea lamprey can be distinguished from other lampreys present in Lake Superior by its dorsal fin, which is separated into two distinct parts. The other species have undivided dorsal fins.

Silver Lamprey, *Ichthyomyzon unicuspis* Hubbs and Trautman

Scientific name: *Ichthyomyzon* = fish to suck (Greek); *unicuspis* = one point (Latin), referring to the presence of one cusp on each of the horny teeth around the mouth.

The silver lamprey is a native, slender, eellike species that reaches a maximum length of about 12 inches. The jawless mouth is surrounded by horny teeth, and those surrounding the mouth are unicuspid, or single pointed. The dorsal fin is continuous, with a notch, but never separated into two distinct parts.

The generic name, *Ichthyomyzon*, translates as fish to suck and describes the feeding habits of the adult silver lamprey. The life cycle of the silver lamprey is similar to that of the sea lamprey; the adults die after they have spawned, the eggs hatch, and the larval ammocoetes spend several years in burrows, filter feeding before metamorphosing into predaceous adults. Silver lampreys are common in the Mississippi, Minnesota, St. Croix, Red, and Rainy rivers. They are also abundant in Lake of the Woods and are present in the Great Lakes drainage.

Silver lampreys prey on native fishes such as catfishes, the northern pike, the suckers, the sturgeons, the paddlefish, and the introduced carp. Where silver and chestnut lampreys occur together, the silver lamprey feeds on fishes larger than the ones the chestnut lamprey feeds on. The native lampreys have not had the disastrous impact on fish populations that the sea lamprey has had. Perhaps the silver and chestnut lampreys and their prey species have evolved together and have become adapted to one another.

Chestnut Lamprey, *Ichthyomyzon castaneus* Girard

Scientific name: *Ichthyomyzon* = fish to suck (Greek); *castaneus* = of chestnut color (Greek).

The chestnut lamprey is similar to the silver lamprey. Its dorsal fin is continuous, but the teeth surrounding its mouth are bicuspid, or double pointed. The trivial name *castaneus* refers to this lamprey's chestnut or grayish brown color.

The chestnut lamprey is also similar in its habits and life cycle to the silver lamprey, but it tends to occupy smaller rivers and streams, such as the St. Croix River north of Taylors Falls and the tributaries of the Red River, Big Fork River, and Rainy River in north-central Minnesota. The prey species of the chestnut lamprey tend to be smaller than those of the silver lamprey, but they include sturgeons, catfishes, and suckers.

Chestnut lamprey

Disc and mouth of chestnut lamprey

American Brook Lamprey, *Lampetra appendix* (DeKay)

Scientific name: *Lampetra* = to lick a rock (Latin); *appendix* = appendage (Latin).

The American brook lamprey is a small and slender nonpredaceous species that seldom reaches a length of more than 8 inches. Its dorsal fin is distinctly separated into two parts similar to those of the sea lamprey. In contrast to the sea lamprey, the buccal cavity of the brook lamprey is small and the teeth are blunt and small. *Lampetra* is an apt generic name because the adults congregate in May in large numbers to spawn and they attach themselves to stones by their suckerlike buccal funnels. The life cycle of the brook lamprey is similar in all respects to that of the other lampreys up to completion of metamorphosis. Brook lampreys spend about five years as filter-feeding ammocoetes. After metamorphosis in the late summer or early fall, the adults do not feed but remain in the stream to spawn the following spring.

The brook lamprey is restricted in Minnesota to the small streams of the southeast, primarily the Root River and its tribu-

Brook lamprey

taries. Early in the century, it was known from several tributaries of the Minnesota River, but it has not been collected from
that drainage since the late 1930s.

Disc and mouth of brook lamprey

Family ACIPENSERIDAE
The Sturgeons

The family Acipenseridae is composed of the sturgeons, primitive fishes that have bony plates on their heads and bodies, sharklike (heterocercal) tails, flattened snouts, and mouths under their heads. Twenty-three kinds are living today. Seven of these live in North America, and the rest live in Europe and Asia. Two kinds, the lake sturgeon and the shovelnose sturgeon, are known in Minnesota. Sturgeons either spend their lives in fresh water or live in the sea and swim up rivers to spawn.

Sturgeons are large and economically important fishes. The white sturgeon of the Pacific Coast of North America reaches a length of nearly 20 feet and a weight of almost a ton. The flesh of sturgeons is valuable as human food, and sturgeon eggs are the primary source of caviar, one of the most famous delicacies in the world. Sturgeons are slow-growing fishes that require many years to reach the age at which they can reproduce. They are also sensitive to pollution and have suffered from dams that impede their spawning runs up rivers. Many sturgeon fisheries have been wiped out or drastically depleted within this century, even in Russia, where sturgeons are the basis of an important and tradition-laden industry.

Lake Sturgeon, *Acipenser fulvescens* Rafinesque

Scientific name: *Acipenser* = sturgeon (Latin);
fulvescens = reddish yellow (Latin).

The lake sturgeon is the biggest fish in Minnesota, where it is known to exceed 200 pounds. One specimen taken (probably netted) in Lake of the Woods in 1911 was reported to weigh 236 pounds, and a 225-pounder was found dead in Rush Lake in

Chisago County in 1947. The currently accepted state hook-and-line record is a 162½-pounder caught in the Rainy River in Koochiching County in 1968. Two 310-pound giants are known from the Great Lakes — one from Lake Superior and one from Lake Michigan.

The lake sturgeon occurs from the Hudson Bay region southward as far as Louisiana. It is known from large rivers and lakes in all drainages in Minnesota, but it is rare today throughout the state. Its decline is due to pollution and exploitation. Lake of the Woods, for example, supported what was perhaps the greatest lake sturgeon population of any lake in the world until the late 1800s. Commercial fishermen who sought the walleye in Lake of the Woods netted lake sturgeons by the ton and had them hauled away and dumped. A source of valuable flesh and caviar was thereby depleted, and the fishery has not recovered to this day.

Young lake sturgeons are reddish brown, with a pale belly. Adults are blackish to greenish yellow on the back and sides. The body is rather thick and is armored with rows of bony plates that almost disappear in old individuals. A small hole, called a spiracle, is present just behind each eye. The other Minnesota sturgeon, the shovelnose sturgeon, is more slender and lacks spiracles.

Equipped with a protrusible mouth under its head and sensitive barbels, or feelers, just in front of its mouth, the lake sturgeon seeks food as it swims along near the bottom with its feelers dragging. When it detects the morsels it finds tasty, such as snails, clams, crayfish, and immature insects, it extends its mouth and sucks them in.

Spawning occurs from April to June in either the shallows of lakes or, more typically, tributary streams. Spawning lake sturgeons leap and splash about noisily and leave the eggs to settle to the bottom and hatch without care. Females 6 feet long have been found to contain 30 pounds of eggs, and spawning females may shed more than a million eggs. Females apparently spawn only once in every 2 or 3 years, however, and the overwhelming majority of the eggs fail to hatch. Lake sturgeons grow slowly and reach sexual maturity only when they are about 20 years old. Their life span can easily exceed a century, and one specimen is reported to have lived 152 years.

Shovelnose Sturgeon, *Scaphirhynchus platorynchus* (Rafinesque)

Scientific name: *Scaphirhynchus* = spade snout (Greek); *platorynchus* = broad snout (Greek).

Known in Minnesota from the lower Mississippi, Minnesota, and St. Croix rivers in the southern half of the state, the shovelnose sturgeon is usually found near the bottom in open, flowing channels. Its range is from the headwaters of the Missouri River system through the Midwest to the Gulf of Mexico around the mouth of the Mississippi. It also lives in New Mexico. It is the most common sturgeon in the Missouri and Mississippi rivers, but it is considerably less common today than it was at the beginning of this century.

A much smaller fish than the lake sturgeon, the shovelnose sturgeon rarely exceeds a length of 3 feet and a weight of 5 pounds in Minnesota, although it is sometimes larger. It is brown on top and white below. Its body is thinner than that of the lake sturgeon and it lacks spiracles. The upper lobe of the tail fin ends in a long, delicate filament that inspired another name, switchtail, for this fish.

The shovelnose sturgeon eats a variety of food items that it sucks from the bottom in a way similar to that used by the lake sturgeon. It spawns in spring, when it migrates into shallow streams. Adults in spawning condition have been observed congregating below the dam at Taylors Falls in Chisago County, where they are blocked from moving farther upstream.

The flesh and caviar of the shovelnose sturgeon are excellent. This fish is netted commercially in the Mississippi south of Minnesota often enough to be marketed, and it commands a lucrative retail price.

Family POLYODONTIDAE
The Paddlefishes

The family Polyodontidae is an ancient group that has only two living species, one in North America and one in China. Paddlefishes are primitive fishes that have a unique and distinctive paddlelike snout. They are large fishes that are slow to mature. They are sensitive to pollution, and their numbers have declined in recent years. The American paddlefish is currently finding refuge in large impoundments in the Midwest.

Painting of paddlefish

Paddlefish, *Polyodon spathula* (Walbaum)

Scientific name: *Polyodon* = many tooth (Greek), apparently referring to the many gill rakers; *spathula* = spatula (Latin).

The paddlefish lives in the lower Mississippi and St. Croix rivers in Minnesota, where it is rare today. It is most common in Lake St. Croix and Lake Pepin. It was formerly more abundant and widely distributed in Minnesota, but its numbers have decreased owing to pollution and heavy commercial fishing in the Mississippi around the beginning of this century. Its range is from the headwaters of the Missouri River system through the Midwest to the Gulf of Mexico.

Readily distinguished from all other Minnesota fishes by its paddlelike snout, the paddlefish is sometimes called the spoonbill or the spoonbill catfish. It is bluish to blackish on the back and sides and white below. It is known to exceed 150 pounds farther south, but apparently it rarely reaches as much as 50 pounds in Minnesota.

Although it attains a large size, the paddlefish feeds mostly on **plankton** (tiny animals and plants that are suspended in the water). Swimming along with its mouth wide open and its snout swinging from side to side, the paddlefish passes great quantities of water through its mouth and out its gills. The prey items are strained out by the long **gill rakers** and swallowed. The role of the snout has long been the subject of speculation. It has been suggested that the snout is used to dig in the bottom, but it is too fragile for digging. The snout is loaded with sense organs and might help the paddlefish locate its food. The flesh and caviar of the paddlefish are excellent. Taking paddlefish is illegal in Minnesota, but they are marketed in the South.

Paddlefish are found in large rivers and river lakes most of the time, but they migrate into streams to spawn over gravel bars in the spring, when the water is high. They have been reported to move several miles upstream for spawning. The newly hatched young lack long snouts, which begin to grow in three weeks. The young grow rapidly, attaining a length of 6 inches by mid-summer.

Family LEPISOSTEIDAE
The Gars

The family Lepisosteidae includes seven kinds of primitive fishes called the gars. Gars live in fresh or brackish water from Canada to Central America. They are easy to recognize by their long, cylindrical bodies and long snouts, which bear numerous sharp teeth. Two kinds of gars, the longnose gar and the short-nose gar, live in Minnesota.

Gars are carnivorous, feeding mostly on smaller fishes, both dead and alive. Because of their feeding habits, gars are generally held in disfavor by anglers in Minnesota. As predators, however, they are useful in controlling the populations of small fishes, thus helping to preserve a natural balance.

Gars are ancient fishes that, despite having changed little over millions of years, are well equipped for survival. They are covered by an armor of bone and heavy scales. A 300-pound gar (the size sometimes reached by the alligator gar in the South) is indeed a formidable fish. Gars are most common in the backwaters of rivers and lakes, where the temperature of the water may become warm and the oxygen supply may become depleted. The gars can come to the surface and gulp air, and they habitually do so. Thus, they can live in water that has so little oxygen that other fishes would die if they stayed. In fact, gars trapped in nets and unable to reach the surface have been known to drown.

Gars occasionally bite on hooks, but they are hard to catch because it is difficult to set a hook in their bony jaws. People in the South have devised special techniques for catching gars, and gars also provide good sport for those who fish with bows. One should not eat gar eggs, because they have been reported to be poisonous. (The authors doubt that this warning is necessary!)

Longnose Gar, *Lepisosteus osseus* (Linnaeus)

Scientific name: *Lepisosteus* = bony scale (Greek); *osseus* = of bone (Latin).

The longnose gar lives in shallow lakes and large rivers and their tributaries in central and southern Minnesota. It commonly inhabits sloughs along the St. Croix, Minnesota, and Mississippi rivers. Its range is from Montana eastward into the St. Lawrence drainage and southward to the Gulf of Mexico.

The longnose gar attains a length of 5 feet in Minnesota but usually is smaller. It is olive green or brown above and white below. Its body and fins have conspicuous black spots. The longnose gar is most easily distinguished from the shortnose gar

Longnose gar

by its snout. The snout of the longnose gar is very long and narrow, about 20 times as long as it is wide. (For this reason, the fish is sometimes called the needlenose gar.) The snout of the shortnose gar is shorter and broader, only about 6 times as long as it is wide.

Small fishes compose most of the diet of the longnose gar. It is seldom eaten by people in Minnesota and so is of little economic use. Gars seem to be uncommon in the good fishing lakes in the state.

The longnose gar spawns in the spring, most often in sloughs and streams. The females are larger than the males and are outnumbered by them. Spawning females are often attended by several males. The large, green eggs settle into the weeds or onto the botton and are abandoned. They hatch in about a week. Young gars are very interesting little animals. They have a black stripe on each side and a pointed upper lobe on the tail fin; the stripes on the sides soon disappear. When they are first hatched, the fish have a disc on their snouts with which they attach themselves to rocks or logs before they start feeding. They eat tiny aquatic animals at first but grow rapidly and soon start eating other fishes. Young gars often float on the surface in groups, where one must look carefully to distinguish them from sticks.

Shortnose Gar, *Lepisosteus platostomus* Rafinesque

Scientific name: *Lepisosteus* = bony scale (Greek);
platostomus = broad mouth (Greek).

The shortnose gar occurs from Montana through the Midwest to the Gulf of Mexico. It is found in shallow lakes and large

Shortnose gar

rivers and their tributaries in central and southern Minnesota, often in the company of the longnose gar.

The shortnose gar is smaller than the longnose gar and rarely reaches a length of 3 feet in Minnesota. It is similar to the long-nose gar in color and is best distinguished from the latter by its shorter, broader snout.

Small fishes are important in the diet of the shortnose gar, but it eats other items, such as crayfish and insects, as well. The shortnose gar spawns in the spring, often in weedy sloughs. Its breeding activities resemble those of the longnose gar.

Family AMIIDAE
The Bowfin

The family Amiidae consists of only one living species, the bowfin of eastern North America. The bowfin is a survivor of an ancient group. It has bony plates around its skull and a bony plate called the gular plate on the bottom of its head. It can gulp air at the surface of the water and so can live in water from which the oxygen has been depleted.

Bowfin, *Amia calva* Linnaeus

Scientific name: *Amia* = a Greek name for some kind of fish; *calva* = smooth (Latin).

Typically an inhabitant of slow-moving water and backwaters, the bowfin lives in lakes and streams over much of Minnesota except for the Hudson Bay and Lake Superior drainages. Its range is from Minnesota to Vermont and southward over much of the eastern United States to the Gulf of Mexico.

The bowfin reaches a weight of about 10 pounds. It is green on the back and sides and white below. The bowfin has a large black spot, known as the eyespot, at the base of the tail. The eyespot is so called because of its appearance and not because it has a sensory function. It fades in adult females.

Generally regarded as a nuisance in Minnesota, where it is often called a dogfish, the bowfin is an aggressive fish that eats a variety of small aquatic animals, especially other fishes. It bites on live bait and plugs and is a strong fighter, but its flesh is of poor quality and it has little value as a food fish.

The bowfin spawns in May and June in Minnesota, when it moves into small streams or weedy bays of lakes. The males, whose fins are bright blue green in the breeding season, clean areas for nests by biting off vegetation and fanning away sediments with their fins. After females have spawned and left, each male guards his nest and the young that hatch. The young school together for several weeks, until they are about 4 inches long, when they disperse and the male abandons them.

Bowfin

Family HIODONTIDAE
The Mooneyes

The family Hiodontidae includes two species, the goldeye and the mooneye, both of which are confined to North America and both of which live in Minnesota. Mooneyes live in lakes and large rivers and are most common in Minnesota in the large, northern lakes, where the goldeye contributes to the commercial catch.

Mooneyes are silvery fish that have large scales, flat-sided bodies, and keeled bellies. They are called mooneyes because of their large, round eyes. Mooneyes resemble herrings and are sometimes called toothed herring. They can be distinguished from herrings by the absence of a saw-toothed edge on the belly; by the presence of at least a partial lateral line; by the presence of well-developed teeth on the jaws, roof of the mouth, and tongue; and by the placement of the anal fin under the dorsal fin, rather than distinctly behind it.

Goldeye, *Hiodon alosoides* (Rafinesque)

Scientific name: *Hiodon* = toothed hyoid (Greek);
alosoides = shadlike (Latin and Greek).

The goldeye lives in lakes and rivers in Minnesota, where it is known from all drainage basins except the Lake Superior drainage. It is most common in large lakes and in quiet places and backwaters of large rivers, such as the Mississippi, Minnesota, and St. Croix and their tributaries. It ranges from the Northwest Territories southward through much of the Midwest into Louisiana and Mississippi.

Bluish above, silvery or yellowish on the sides, and silvery or white below, the goldeye is a shiny fish that reaches a length of about a foot in Minnesota. As its common name suggests, the eyes are gold colored. The belly has a sharp keel (but is not saw-toothed) from the anal fin to the pectoral fins. The goldeye resembles the mooneye, but it can be distinguished from the latter by its having a longer keel on the belly; by its having the front of the dorsal fin about even with the front of the anal fin, rather than distinctly ahead of it; and by its having 9 or 10 rays in the dorsal fin, in contrast to the mooneye's 11 or 12.

A variety of aquatic animals, including insects, crayfish, snails, and small fishes, serve as food for the goldeye. It feeds most actively in the evening and at night, often at or near the surface of the water. It bites occasionally on live or artificial baits. It is unimportant as a sport fish in Minnesota, but it has commercial value in Lake of the Woods and the Red Lakes. Smoked goldeye is a popular dish in some places in Canada and northern Minnesota.

The goldeye spawns in May and June in Minnesota. It migrates into shallow tributaries of lakes and rivers, and females shed their eggs randomly on the bottom. The young that hatch remain in the tributaries until late summer, when they move downstream into the lake or river from which their parents came.

Mooneye, *Hiodon tergisus* LeSueur

Scientific name: *Hiodon* = toothed hyoid (Greek); *tergisus* = polished (Greek).

The mooneye is known from lakes and rivers in much of Minnesota except the Lake Superior drainage. It is most often found in quiet places and in backwaters of large lakes and rivers

Mooneye

and frequently in association with the goldeye. It ranges from the Hudson Bay region of Canada southward through the Ohio Valley into Mississippi.

The mooneye is similar in size and color to the goldeye, but the former's eye is silvery rather than gold. The keel on its belly is shorter than that of the goldeye, extending only from the anal fin to the pelvic fins. The front of the dorsal fin is distinctly in front of the anal fin and contains 11 or 12 rays.

The feeding and spawning habits of the mooneye are similar to those of the goldeye. The mooneye is sometimes caught by commercial fishermen in northern lakes, such as Lake of the Woods and the Red Lakes, but, because its flesh is dry and tasteless, it is regarded as a poor food fish of little commercial value.

Family CLUPEIDAE
The Herrings

The family Clupeidae consists of the herrings, most of which are ocean fishes. Some herrings swim up freshwater streams to spawn. Others, including the two kinds found in Minnesota (the alewife and the gizzard shad) can live their entire lives in fresh water. The alewife recently reached the Minnesota region through the Great Lakes, and the gizzard shad is a natural resident. A third herring, the skipjack, is also native to Minnesota but has apparently been eliminated from the state in this century by dams that block its migration route in the Mississippi River.

Herrings are silvery, flat-sided fishes that have a row of specialized, saw-toothed scales running along the edges of their bellies. Their eyes are covered by transparent, slit membranes called adipose eyelids. Some herrings are among the most important food fishes taken from the sea. The freshwater kinds are less valued for food and can, in fact, become nuisances because of their capacity to become extremely abundant when conditions are favorable. They are useful as food for larger fishes, however, and the gizzard shad is vital as a source of food for game fishes in large reservoirs in the South.

Alewife, *Alosa pseudoharengus* (Wilson)

Scientific name: *Alosa* = shad (Latin);
pseudoharengus = false herring (Greek).

A native of the Atlantic Ocean that can live in fresh water, the alewife reached Minnesota through the Great Lakes. It lived in Lake Ontario for many years and probably gained access to the remaining Great Lakes through the Welland Canal between Lake Ontario and Lake Erie. It was first found in the Minnesota waters of Lake Superior in 1956.

The alewife is a silvery fish, usually less than a foot long, that has a purple spot on each side behind its head. It is slimmer than the gizzard shad and can be distinguished from the latter by its lack of an elongated ray at the back of the dorsal fin. It feeds chiefly on tiny aquatic animals that it filters from the water. It is used for food in the eastern United States but is not particularly tasty. Alewives spawn in the shallows of lakes or in tributary streams. Spawning is carried out by schooling adults as they swim near the surface. Eggs are shed in the open water, settle to the bottom, and develop without parental care.

A prolific fish that can become overabundant, the alewife is subject to annual crashes in which sudden, massive die-offs occur. These die-offs occur in the summer and seem to be triggered by warm water temperatures. Summerkills of alewives are extensive and, therefore, troublesome in Lake Michigan. In Lake Michigan, the alewife competes for food with the lake herring (tullibee), which is a desirable commercial fish there. After the coming of the alewife, the catch of lake herring declined. The summerkills in Lake Michigan result in alewives being washed onto beaches by the ton, creating a nuisance that is expensive to remove. Predation by the lake trout used to control the alewife in Lake Ontario, but the lake trout has decreased in the Great Lakes due to pollution and the presence of the sea lamprey, another invader from the Atlantic. The coho salmon has been introduced into the Great Lakes to control the alewife. The coho is a desirable fish that has adapted remarkably well in Lake Michigan, although its presence could inhibit the rehabilitation of the lake trout there.

As evidenced by the alewife, human activities have indeed wrought significant effects on the balance of nature in Lake Michigan. The alewife has not become the problem in the Minnesota portion of Lake Superior that it has in Lake Michigan and probably never will. The lack of broad, shallow areas in Lake Superior and the presence of waterfalls on the North Shore streams seem to limit the success of its spawning runs, thereby helping to control the population. The relatively cool temperature of Lake Superior reduces the likelihood of summerkills. Alewives are caught by commercial fishermen in Lake Superior but compose only a minor part of the catch.

Gizzard shad

Gizzard Shad, *Dorosoma cepedianum* (LeSueur)

Scientific name: *Dorosoma* = lance body (Greek); *cepedianum* = named for Comte de Lacépède, a French naturalist.

The gizzard shad lives in lakes and large rivers over the southern half of Minnesota. It is most common in quiet water, including the backwaters of the Mississippi, Minnesota, and St. Croix rivers and their tributaries. Its range is from the Missouri River system in North Dakota eastward into the St. Lawrence drainage and southward to Mexico.

The gizzard shad reaches a length of a foot or more. It is silvery, with a bluish back. The young have a purple spot on each side, but this fades in adults. In adults the lower jaw is short and fits into a notch in the upper jaw. A distinctive characteristic is the greatly elongated last ray of the dorsal fin.

An active fish that often travels in schools, the gizzard shad filters tiny aquatic plants and animals from the water for food. Gizzard shad sometimes skip along the surface. They spawn in the spring in shallow water. Eggs are shed into the open water and develop without parental care.

When small, the gizzard shad is useful as food for other fishes. It is the most important food for basses and crappies in some reservoirs in the South. It grows rapidly, however, and soon becomes too big for other fishes to eat. It is not popular as food for people, but it can be processed as a source of fertilizer, oil, and animal feed.

The gizzard shad is named for Comte de Lacépède (1756–1825), a French naturalist who wrote early books on the classification of fishes and reptiles and was active in politics in the days of Napoleon Bonaparte.

Family ANGUILLIDAE
The Freshwater Eels

The family Anguillidae includes the freshwater eels, which are well known for their long, snakelike shape. Freshwater eels are **catadromous,** that is, they actually hatch in the sea and migrate into fresh water, where they live for several years before returning to the sea again to spawn and, apparently, to die. This family is widely distributed and includes about 16 species, only 1 of which, the American eel, enters fresh water in North America. Minnesota is included in its range.

American Eel, *Anguilla rostrata* (LeSueur)

Scientific name: *Anguilla* = eel (Latin);
rostrata = beaked (Latin).

The American eel is native to rivers of the lower Mississippi River system in Minnesota. Although rare today, it is found occasionally in the Mississippi, St. Croix, and Minnesota rivers. It has recently appeared in the Minnesota waters of Lake Superior, presumably after gaining access to the western Great Lakes through the St. Lawrence Seaway. Its range includes the western North Atlantic and streams from Greenland through eastern North America and eastern Central America.

To reach Minnesota in the Mississippi system, the American eel must complete an arduous and remarkable journey of more than 2,000 miles. American eels are hatched in the Atlantic, apparently near or in the region called the Sargasso Sea. The newly hatched young are tiny, transparent, and leaflike; and they show no obvious resemblance to adult eels. These young drift toward North and Central America along ocean currents and reach coastal waters after about a year. There they complete the process of changing into a form recognizable as small eels and begin swimming up streams and rivers. They must overcome all barriers — such as pollution, dams, and waterfalls — that block their way. An eel in Lake St. Croix today passed 29 dams on its long trip up from the mouth of the Mississippi. Eels get past these dams by traveling through their locks. After several years in inland waters, adult eels complete their odyssey by migrating downstream to their spawning grounds in the sea, where they reproduce. Spawning has not been observed, but it may take place deep beneath the surface. Adults are thought to die after they spawn.

It has long been said that only female American eels migrate far into fresh water and that males stay near the mouths of rivers for most of their lives. This idea has been challenged recently with the suggestion that one cannot readily determine the sex of American eels for most of their time in fresh water, so that males might be among those that ascend the rivers. Females reach a length of 4 feet and males 1½ feet. Large females weigh up to 7 pounds.

Eels are long and cylindrical, and they are slimy because they secrete a great deal of mucus (hence the phrase slippery as an eel). They have pectoral fins but lack pelvic fins. Adults are typically brownish above and whitish below, but those migrating seaward to spawn turn bronze or blackish above and may turn silvery below. Eels resemble lampreys in shape but can be distinguished by their having jaws, unlike the jawless, disclike mouths of lampreys.

Eels are most active at night, when they feed voraciously on various aquatic animals, such as small fishes, immature insects, crayfish, snails, and worms. In the day, they hide under cover or lie buried in mud. Apparently, they also bury themselves in mud in cold winter weather.

Eel flesh is not a popular dish in Minnesota, but it is highly regarded in the eastern United States and Europe. Commercially caught eels can be cooked, smoked, pickled, or jellied. Smoking is by far the most popular method of preparation.

Family ESOCIDAE
The Pikes

The family Esocidae includes the pikes and the pickerels, which are familiar, carnivorous fishes that are easily recognized by their long, duckbill-shaped jaws lined with sharp teeth. Their bodies are elongated and streamlined for quick movements. Pikes typically lurk in concealment and capture their prey by making a sudden dash. Thus, the best fishing technique for pikes is casting or trolling around weed beds and stumps in shallow water.

Pikes live in Europe, Asia, and North America. Five species are living today. Only two of these, the northern pike and the muskellunge, live in Minnesota, but these two are extremely important as game fishes and as predators that control the populations of smaller fishes. The northern pike is one of the most commonly caught sport fishes in Minnesota, and the muskellunge offers a challenge that attracts anglers from near and far.

Northern pike

Northern Pike, *Esox lucius* Linnaeus

Scientific name: *Esox* = pike (Latin); *lucius* = Latin name for this species.

The most widely distributed freshwater fish in the world, the northern pike includes much of northern North America, Europe, and Asia in its range. In North America, it occurs as far south as Missouri and has been introduced in several places outside its natural range. It is common throughout most of Minnesota's lakes, rivers, and streams. It is most often found around aquatic vegetation in quiet or slow-moving water.

A carnivorous fish whose diet consists mostly of other fishes, the northern pike bites readily on spoons, plugs, and minnows. Although sometimes scorned by anglers who seek other game fishes, the northern is one of the most valuable sport fishes in Minnesota because it is large, easy to catch, and good to eat. The world record for hook-and-line northerns is a specimen of 46 pounds, 2 ounces, caught in the Sacandaga Reservoir in New York in 1940. The Minnesota record is 45 pounds, 12 ounces.

The northern pike is greenish above and white below. Young northerns have light bars on their sides. These bars break into irregular spots in adults. A strain of northern pike called the silver pike, which is silvery or grayish and lacks distinct markings, occurs in northern Minnesota.

The only other Minnesota fish that resembles the northern pike closely is the muskellunge. Whereas the northern has pale markings on a dark background, the muskellunge, when marked, has dark markings on a light background. The V-shaped tail of the northern is less pointed than that of the muskellunge. The northern also has 10 or fewer pores under its jaws, whereas the muskellunge has 11 to 18 (Figure 40). Northerns and muskellunge sometimes interbreed to produce hybrids that are intermediate between the parental species in appearance. The northern is sometimes called the snake pickerel in Minnesota, but pickerel is used properly for other smaller kinds of pikes.

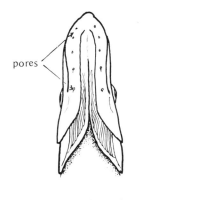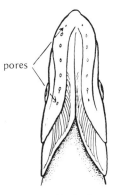

a. Northern pike   b. Muskellunge

Figure 40. Pores under jaws of (a) the northern pike and (b) the muskellunge.

The northern pike spawns in April and May in Minnesota soon after the previous winter's ice melts. Adults move into tributary streams, flooded lowlands, and shallows of lakes to spawn. Eggs are shed randomly and hatch in about two weeks. The young eat tiny aquatic animals at first and soon begin eating other small fishes. Young northerns and muskellunge turn to cannibalism quickly when other food is not sufficient.

Because they hatch in tributaries and temporarily flooded places, young northerns are in danger of being stranded away from adjoining lakes when water levels drop. As a key part of its program of managing the northern pike, the Minnesota DNR has 150 spawning areas in which the water is held at appropriate levels by control gates. About 4 million northerns are produced in these areas annually. The DNR also harvests northerns from winterkill lakes by using an interesting technique. When the oxygen in the water decreases, pumps are used to create well-oxygenated currents, thus attracting northerns to traps. These fish can then be introduced elsewhere.

Muskellunge

Muskellunge, *Esox masquinongy* Mitchill

Scientific name: *Esox* = pike (Latin);
masquinongy = Indian name for this species.

The muskellunge is the aristocrat of Minnesota's trophy fishes. It is a large and ferocious predator whose size, fighting strength, wariness, and unpredictability provide an exciting test of an angler's skill. The muskie is most common in Minnesota in clear, northern lakes, such as Lake of the Woods, Rainy Lake, Leech Lake, and Lake Winnibigoshish. It also inhabits large rivers, such as the Rainy and the Mississippi. Its range is from central Canada eastward into the St. Lawrence drainage and southward into Tennessee. It prefers clear water and is often found around beds of aquatic vegetation, especially pondweed.

Dedicated muskie anglers work many hours and use all the techniques and tricks at their command to outwit the wily muskie; yet, some go for years without ever catching one. Muskie anglers use heavy tackle and plugs, spoons, and suckers as big as a foot long for bait. A popular approach is to pull the bait through the water as fast as possible in a zigzag pattern in an attempt to excite a muskie into striking incautiously. Muskies are famous for following the bait and then, apparently uninterested, turning away as the lure approaches the angler. Once hooked, muskies fight savagely, leaping out of the water as they try to shake the hook. The world record for a hook-and-line muskie is a specimen of 69 pounds, 15 ounces, that was caught in the St. Lawrence River in 1957. The Minnesota record is 54 pounds.

Muskies occasionally go on sprees in which they bite more readily than usual. In the most famous "muskie rampage" in the annals of Minnesota fishing, more than 160 muskies weighing between 15 and 43 pounds were caught within two weeks in July of 1955 in Leech Lake in Cass County. The cause of such anglers' dreams is not known, but the sprees typically occur during periods of hot weather. It has been suggested that the big fish simply go crazy with the heat. In the Leech Lake muskie rampage, apparently agitated muskies often were seen at the surface. They struck viciously at any bait tossed near them.

Muskies vary in color, but most Minnesota muskies are silver muskies, silvery to greenish fish that have dark stripes and spots along their sides. The stripes fade in large specimens. Muskies from the area of Lake of the Woods are brownish and usually lack stripes. The northern pike resembles the muskie but has pale markings on a dark background, rather than dark markings on a light background.

The muskellunge spawns in May in Minnesota, typically in tributary streams or shallows near the margins of lakes. Females shed their eggs randomly. Muskies spawn later than northerns. This timing creates a disadvantage for the young muskies, because northerns hatched the same spring have a head start in growth and may eat many of the tiny muskies in their first few weeks of life. Newly hatched muskies also have a habit of floating on the surface, where they are subject to predation by birds and to death due to rapid warming of the water on hot summer days.

Muskies are carnivorous throughout their lives, and the newly hatched young eat tiny aquatic animals. They grow rapidly and soon begin eating other fishes. They reach a length of about 6 inches by the end of their first summer. The Minnesota DNR is carrying on a successful program of hatching muskies, rearing them through their first summer, and then stocking them in selected lakes and streams.

Family UMBRIDAE
The Mudminnows

The family Umbridae is composed of small, hardy, heavy-bodied fishes commonly called mudminnows. Five species are living today. Four of these live in North America, but only one, the central mudminnow, lives in Minnesota.

Mudminnows are poorly named in the sense that they are not minnows at all but form their own group. They are well named, however, in the sense that they burrow in mud, a habit that helps account for their ability to survive in places where some fishes cannot live. Mudminnows characteristically inhabit slug-

Mudminnow

gish streams and stagnant pools and ponds. These habitats are vulnerable to oxygen depletion, and mudminnows can gulp oxygen from the air. Mudminnows also survive in highly acidic bogs and in ponds that are mostly frozen in winter. By burrowing, they can even survive periods of dryness when their ponds nearly dry out.

Central Mudminnow, *Umbra limi* (Kirtland)

Scientific name: *Umbra* = a shade (Latin), possibly referring to a dark habitat; *limi* = mud (Latin).

Widely distributed in Minnesota, the central mudminnow occurs in all of the state's drainage systems. It is most common in cool bogs, ditches, weedy ponds, and sluggish streams in the northern and central parts of the state. Its range is from the St. Lawrence region westward through the Great Lakes basin and central United States into Ontario and Manitoba.

Well camouflaged for its bottom-dwelling habits, the central mudminnow is brownish above, mottled brown on the sides, and whitish below. Adults have a distinct vertical bar just in front of the tail fin. The tail fin is rounded. The central mudminnow grows as long as 8 inches in Minnesota, but most individuals are about half that size. Mudminnows eat mostly vegetation and small aquatic animals, such as worms and insects. They also eat small fishes, especially when the latter are trapped in ponds with them when water levels drop.

Because of its habits, the central mudminnow is a relatively unfamiliar fish. When threatened, it quickly burrows, tail first, into the mud and so is hard to catch. Even so, it is used occasionally as a bait fish in Minnesota.

Despite its ability to thrive in habitats that have a soft bottom of natural ooze and muck, the central mudminnow apparently does not adapt well to the presence of silt over the bottom or to turbidity. It has decreased in places where siltation, drainage of lowlands, and destruction of aquatic vegetation have occurred.

The central mudminnow spawns in the late spring in Minnesota. Females deposit their eggs singly on vegetation, where the eggs stick. The young hatch about a week after fertilization.

Family SALMONIDAE
The Salmons

The family Salmonidae contains more important game fishes than any other family of fishes found in Minnesota. Some of the most valuable commercial fishes in the Northern Hemisphere belong to this family. The Salmonidae includes the whitefishes, ciscoes, trouts, graylings, and chars in addition to the well-known salmons. All the members of the family have an adipose fin on their backs between the dorsal and tail fins. The function of the adipose fin is unknown, but the presence of the fin in other distantly related fish families suggests that it may have some functional significance. Another feature of the salmonids is the axillary process, a scalelike structure near the anterior dorsal margin of the pelvic fin; its function is also uncertain. All the members of the family are inhabitants of cold waters, usually less than 72° F, and they are commonly called cold-water fishes. Many (for example, salmons and steelheads) are anadromous, that is, they enter rivers and streams to spawn. Because of their quality as sport fishes, many of the species of Salmonidae have been widely introduced throughout the world, including the mountainous regions of Africa, South America, and New Zealand.

Sportfishing in Lake Superior and Lake Michigan is a thriving industry, an industry more valuable than the commercial fishery of the early decades of this century. Fishing for salmon and trout in Lake Superior requires special preparation, except in the autumn when the fishes are beginning their spawning run. Large boats and motors are a must. Professional guides are important to success, and special deep-sea fishing equipment is essential. Sonar is used to locate the fishes (some guides may actually be able to identify the species appearing as a blip on the chart paper), and special weighted lines and outriggers are used to get the lures, spoons, spinners, and plugs down to the fishes, which in midsummer may be at depths of 50 to 100 feet.

Arctic Grayling, *Thymallus arcticus* (Pallas)

Scientific name: *Thymallus* = Greek name for this genus, referring to a supposed odor of thyme; *arcticus* = of the arctic.

The Arctic grayling reaches a length of 18 inches or more. The most striking characteristic of the Arctic grayling is its long, high, saillike dorsal fin. The dorsal fin is dark gray, with rows of blue or violet spots set off by light borders, and its upper margin is bright red. The body is iridescent violet gray and silver and is covered with small spots.

As its name suggests, this fish is common to Arctic waters. Two isolated relict populations once existed in the United States, however. One was in Michigan's upper peninsula and a few streams in lower Michigan, and the other was in the upper Missouri River in Montana. About 30 years ago, Arctic grayling were introduced into several lakes in the Arrowhead region of Minnesota. The latter population was maintained until recently by continued stocking.

The Arctic grayling is one of the finest game fishes, but it is not as wary as many other species of the salmon family are. Arctic grayling can be taken with both wet and dry flies and with small spinners.

Pink Salmon, *Oncorhynchus gorbuscha* (Walbaum)

Scientific name: *Oncorhynchus* = hooked snout (Greek); *gorbuscha* = old Russian name for this species.

The pink salmon was accidentally introduced into Lake Superior in 1956. These fish subsequently spawned successfully in tributary streams, and their progeny established a self-sustaining population in the lake. Pink salmon spawn in their second year of life and, as do all Pacific salmons, die after they are spawned out. The eggs hatch the following spring, and the young **fry** drift back to Lake Superior. Their period of growth in the lake is quite rapid, 18 months long, and they reach a weight of 2 to 4 pounds at maturity. The Minnesota hook-and-line record for the pink salmon is 2 pounds, 13 ounces.

The numbers of pink salmon that spawn in odd-numbered years are greater than the numbers that spawn in even-numbered years. In the autumn of 1979, several North Shore streams, including the Cascade, Devil Track, and Brule rivers, had such large numbers of spawning pink salmon that every available gravel riffle was occupied by 20 or 30 pairs of fish. The run was comparable to the famous pink salmon runs in the North Pacific coastal streams of British Columbia and Alaska.

Young pink salmon can be distinguished from young coho salmon and chinook salmon by the absence of parr marks (vertical bars or stripes on the sides of the young of some trouts and salmons). Spawning male pink salmon develop large hooks, or kypes, on their upper jaws and large humps on their backs just behind their heads.

The trivial names of all the Pacific salmons found in North America are based on old Russian vernacular names given the various species, for example, *gorbuscha*. A German surgeon-naturalist, Wilhelm Stellar, who was associated with the Dane Vitus Bering's Siberian and Kamchatka (1742 to 1744) explorations, is credited with collecting and identifying all the species of Pacific salmon. Stellar died before he could publish his findings. In 1792 the German ichthyologist Johann Walbaum published descriptions of the species and used the names that Stellar had used in his detailed field notes.

Coho Salmon, *Oncorhynchus kisutch* (Walbaum)

Scientific name: *Oncorhynchus* = hooked snout (Greek); *kisutch* = old Russian name for this species.

The coho salmon was first introduced into Lake Superior and Lake Michigan by the Michigan Department of Conservation in 1965. The initial stocking was successful, and a year later coho salmon were caught by anglers. Today, salmons, especially the coho and chinook, have become sport fishes more important in the upper Great Lakes than even the native lake trout. The stocking program of the Minnesota Department of Natural Resources has had less spectacular success than that of Michigan, but it has contributed to the revitalization of the deep-sea sport-fishing destroyed by the predaceous sea lamprey.

The coho salmon has a metallic blue back, and the sides of its body and belly are silvery. The dorsal fin and upper lobe of the tail fin are covered with spots. The flesh along the base of the teeth in the lower jaw is not pigmented. Young coho salmon have parr marks, and their adipose fins are uniformly pig-mented.

Coho salmon are autumn spawners and enter tributary streams in the third year of their lives. The mature males de-velop reddish pigment on their bodies and their bellies darken. Males also develop pronounced hooks on their jaws. Mature females begin construction of nests, or redds, from early Octo-ber to November and then are joined by the males shortly after nest construction begins. During the courtship and spawning, there is a lot of chasing and splashing, and it often looks like every square foot of a gravel riffle is occupied by mating fish. The female lays a number of eggs, which are fertilized by the attending male. The female then moves upstream to the upper edge of the nest and fans out a new depression. The pebbles, sand, and gravel scooped by her body and tail settle down downstream, covering the eggs she released. Egg laying begins again, the eggs are fertilized and settle to the bottom, and the female moves upstream and constructs another nest. The proc-ess is repeated until she is spent. The male and female then die, and their bodies are carried downstream. The eggs in the gravel hatch the following spring. The larval fish, **alevins,** live at first on the yolk provided in their yolk sacs. Shortly thereafter, the larval fish emerge from the gravel and begin to feed on algae. They grow rapidly and soon begin feeding on microscopic ani-mals as well.

Young coho salmon remain in the nursery stream during their first year of life and then migrate to Lake Superior or Lake Michigan the following year. In their remaining two years of life, they feed actively in the lake, grow rapidly, and reach weights of 25 pounds or more before they return to the rivers and streams to spawn. Minnesota streams tributary to Lake Su-perior are not well suited for coho spawning for several reasons;

this fact explains the Minnesota stocking program's lack of success. The North Shore streams have impassable barriers very near their mouths, and the short segments of stream available offer few of the gravel riffles that are required for the successful spawning and hatching of the eggs. Low water levels in the autumn prevent the movement of salmon from the lake upstream, and, by the time stream flows increase and the barrier bars are breached, the water tempratures are so low (39° F) that the fish do not spawn. The streams on the south shore of Lake Superior in Michigan and Wisconsin are more suitable, as are large streams in Ontario east of Thunder Bay. The world record for a hook-and-line coho for inland lakes is a specimen of 24 pounds, 6 ounces, caught in Lake Michigan in 1975. The Minnesota record is 10 pounds, 6½ ounces.

Chinook Salmon, *Oncorhynchus tshawytscha* (Walbaum)

Scientific name: *Oncorhynchus* = hooked snout (Greek); *tshawytscha* = old Russian name for this species.

The chinook salmon is another important and successful introduction into Lake Superior and Lake Michigan. As early as 1876, unsuccessful attempts were made by the United States Fish Commission to introduce the chinook salmon into the lakes in south-central and east-central Minnesota. Years later, attempts by the same commission to introduce salmon into Lake Superior met with no better success. In 1967, Michigan fishery biologists introduced chinook salmon **fingerlings** into the Huron River, a tributary to Lake Superior. Their introduction was a success, and with continued stocking the chinook salmon has become an important addition to the sport fishery.

The chinook salmon, or king salmon, is the largest and most desirable of the Pacific salmon species. Specimens can reach a weight of more than 100 pounds, but most weigh closer to 20 pounds. The world record for a hook-and-line chinook for inland lakes is a specimen of 41 pounds, 8 ounces, that was caught in Lake Michigan in 1976. The Minnesota record is 23 pounds, 6¾ ounces.

The chinook salmon has a dusky back and silvery sides; there are numerous black spots on its back, and its dorsal and tail fins are heavily spotted. The flesh along the base of the teeth in the lower jaw is black. Young chinook salmon have parr marks, and there is a clear area (window) in the adipose fin.

Chinook salmon usually mature in their fourth or fifth year of life, but some fish may take up to seven years to mature. The spawning behavior of the chinook salmon is similar to that of the pink salmon and the coho salmon. The adults die shortly after spawning. The young fry may remain in the river or stream until they are one or two years old before migrating downstream to a lake or the ocean.

Brook trout. Photo by Dr. Don Beimborn.

Brook Trout, *Salvelinus fontinalis* (Mitchill)

Scientific name: *Salvelinus* = an old name for char, from the same root as the German *Saibling,* a little salmon; *fontinalis* = living in springs (Latin).

The brook trout is the most attractive of all the salmonids. It has a dark olive back, with light marbled streaks. The sides are dark olive to silver, sprinkled with lighter spots and red spots with light brown margins. The coloration of the brook trout is quite variable. Some fish from the dark brown waters of beaver ponds may be almost coal black; their bellies may be streaked with black pigment, with the red dots on the sides being the only visible spots. Brook trout from lakes or from the mouths of North Shore streams tributary to Lake Superior may be iridescent silver and the red spots may be less prominent. The scales on brook trout are minute and give the fish the appearance of being scaleless. The anal and tail fins have the ventral margins strongly marked by a white to creamy streak. The world record for a hook-and-line trout is a 14-pound, 8-ounce, specimen caught in the Nipigon River in Ontario in 1916. The Minnesota record is 6 pounds, 2 ounces.

Mature males develop a hook on the tip of their lower jaws in the autumn prior to spawning. Brook trout spawn from October to December, congregating in shallow riffles over gravel and rubble bottoms. The female constructs a nest, or redd, by sweeping out a depression in the gravel with her anal and tail fins. A male attends the female as she lays some eggs, fertilizing them as they are released into the water. The fertilized eggs settle to the bottom into the crevices between the gravel and rubble. The process is repeated until the female is spent. During the height of spawning activity, large numbers of breeding fish are present, and there is great competition between the courting males. There is chasing, mock combat, and displaying, and the frenzied activity may make the shallow water seem to boil.

The eggs hatch in the gravel, and the larval fish remain for a time in the gravel. The fry swim up from the gravel and establish territories that they defend from other intruding fry.

The brook trout has been widely introduced throughout northern North America and Europe. Its native range was from the Great Lakes region northward into Manitoba and eastward to Labrador and southward through the Appalachians to Georgia. In Minnesota, the brook trout was native to a few spring-fed streams in the extreme southeast, the spring-fed streams of the upper St. Croix River, and Lake Superior and its tributaries up to the first impassable barrier falls. Early settlers reported that brook trout were native to several lakes above Beaver Bay and Grand Marais. After lumbering began in the pineries of northeastern Minnesota, the loggers stocked any suitable-looking stream. A vast majority of these introductions were undocumented and known only to the walking boss or the logging superintendent. Many of the spring-fed streams and spring holes in the headwaters of the Cloquet and Whiteface rivers along the General Logging Railroad grade were stocked, and they support trout populations today. When he was a young lad, one of the authors (JCU) was taken on a camping trip up the old Vermilion Trail, St. Louis County Highway 4, and caught trout more than 12 inches long in a small stream that had been stocked by the walking boss with two cans of fry brought up on a logging train from Cloquet. Since that day, every cold-water, "trouty looking" stream has been mentally noted as a place for some future adventure.

Today, brook trout are found in cold-water streams throughout the state. These fish are the result of stockings by the DNR in streams previously surveyed by biologists and found to provide suitable habitat for this trout. Many of these introductions have resulted in self-sustaining populations, but annual stocking is required in other streams to maintain a sport fishery.

Brook trout are, in the estimation of many trout anglers, the most prized of fishes. They are wary but vulnerable to the experienced angler, and the habitat in which they live is wild, usually away from the more civilized surroundings of the rainbow trout and the brown trout. In the streams along the North Shore of Lake Superior, the brook trout is in the company of the moose, the black bear, and the otter. It is delicious, the finest of trout.

Lake Trout, *Salvelinus namaycush* (Walbaum)

Scientific name: *Salvelinus* = an old name for char, from the same root as the German *Saibling*, a little salmon; *namaycush* = Indian name for this species, meaning tyrant of the lakes.

The lake trout is found from Alaska eastward across Canada and through the Great Lakes region to the northern New England states. In Minnesota, the lake trout is native to the deep, cold border lakes in northern St. Louis, Lake, and Cook counties and has been introduced into a few lakes in Koochiching and Itasca counties and into Grindstone Lake in Pine County. It once was abundant in Lake Superior. Along with other salmonids, it

Lake trout

has been introduced in the Rocky Mountain region and into European lakes.

The lake trout is the largest of all native North American trout. The world hook-and-line record is a 65-pounder caught in Great Bear Lake in the Northwest Territories in 1970. The Minnesota record is 43 pounds, 8 ounces. Most specimens in inland Minnesota lakes achieve weights of 8 to 12 pounds.

The coloration of the lake trout varies considerably, from a silvery slate gray to almost-black back that shades to gray or grayish white on the belly. The body lacks brightly colored spots but is covered with whitish spots that extend over the unpaired fins. The tail fin is deeply forked. The scales are small but more evident than those of the brook trout. Early fishermen on Isle Royale in Lake Superior recognized at least 10 different kinds of lake trout, attesting to the variability of this species.

The lake trout was once a very important commercial fish in the upper Great Lakes, but it declined after the appearance of the sea lamprey and eventually disappeared in Lake Michigan. In 1942, the commercial catch of lake trout in the United States waters of Lake Superior was 3 million pounds. Within a few years, the lamprey had so depleted the stock that it was no longer profitable for fishermen to operate. The national governments of Canada and the United States have cooperated in trying to control the lamprey populations and reestablish lake trout populations in Lake Superior. Their efforts have resulted in populations of lake trout in the lake, which now can support a sport fishery. It is improbable, however, that commercial fishing for lake trout will develop in the foreseeable future.

Siscowet, *Salvelinus siscowet* (Agassiz)

Scientific name: *Salvelinus* = an old name for char, from the same root as the German *Saibling*, a little salmon; *siscowet* = Indian name for this species.

The siscowet is similar to the lake trout in coloration, but the siscowet is darker and has slightly larger spots on its sides and fins. The siscowet is also deeper bodied: the ratio of body depth to body length is 3.1 to 3.8 in the siscowet and 4.1 to 4.8 in the lake trout. The siscowet also contains far more fat and oil (48.5 percent of its total body weight) than the lake trout (9.4 percent). Commercial fishermen used fat trout and lean trout to describe the two species. Fat trout were unpalatable when eaten fresh but were considered a great delicacy when salted. Apparently, salted fat trout were sold at a premium over lake trout.

In 1850, Prof. Louis Agassiz in his classic book, *Lake Superior*, first described the siscowet as *Salmo siscowet*. He noted that it was "a fish of high and rich flavor, but so fat as to be almost unfit for food, the greater part of it melting down . . . in the process of cooking." Describing the siscowet, Agassiz wrote, "The inhabitants of the region designate it under the name *Siscowet*, a name which I have thought should be preserved in scientific nomenclature." After Agassiz's description, a revision of the trout group led to a separation of the chars from the trouts and the generic name *Salvelinus* replaced *Salmo*.

Rainbow Trout, *Salmo gairdneri* Richardson

Scientific name: *Salmo* = from *salio*, meaning to leap (Latin); *gairdneri* = named for Meredith Gairdner, an early American naturalist.

The rainbow trout was introduced into the Great Lakes from its native range in the western United States. It is bluish or olive green above and silvery on the sides. One of its more obvious characteristics is its broad pink to crimson lateral stripe. The dorsal and tail fins are profusely dotted with small dark spots. Coloration of the rainbow varies considerably, depending on the habitat. Individuals living in lakes, especially Lake Superior,

Juvenile rainbow trout

tend to be colored iridescent silver and their crimson lateral bands may be less prominent than in individuals from rivers and streams.

Some western varieties of the rainbow may weigh up to 50 pounds, but the rainbows in the Great Lakes and in Minnesota are smaller. In Lake Superior and a few inland lakes, rainbows can reach a weight of 15 pounds, but those in streams rarely weigh more than 5 pounds. The world record for a hook-and-line rainbow for inland waters is a 19-pound, 8-ounce, specimen caught in Avington Fishery, United Kingdom, in 1977. The Minnesota record is 17 pounds, 6 ounces.

Rainbow trout. Photo by Dr. Don Beimborn.

Rainbows are migratory fish that live in small streams for the first two or three years of life and then migrate downstream. This migratory behavior has made it difficult for fishery biologists to manage rainbow trout populations for sport. Biologists have recently determined that rainbows in Valley Creek in east-central Minnesota did not migrate in a period of two and one-half years.

Along the North Shore, the rainbows migrate to Lake Superior. Unless they are caught, they grow rapidly and, when mature, migrate into the tributary streams to spawn. Most rainbows migrate in the spring, but a few migrate in the autumn and remain in the stream until the following spring. These migrations, especially the spring ones, provide an opportunity for the angler to catch large fish that are usually only available to fishermen trolling in deep water in Lake Superior or Lake Michigan. Tracking of rainbows by means of transmitters attached to, or implanted in, adults has indicated that individual fish may migrate along the coastline and enter several streams prior to selecting one in which to spawn. Which qualities of a stream determine its suitability for spawning are still a mystery. Anglers attest to the fact that certain streams, for example, the Brule River in Wisconsin and the Baptism and Brule rivers in Minnesota, tend to yield more and larger fish than do other apparently similar streams.

Rainbows are among the hardiest of the trouts and survive at temperatures that are lethal to other species. Considerable research and effort has gone into the development of genetic varieties of rainbows that are hardier, nonmigratory, and faster growing. The Donaldson variety, named for its originator, represents one success in developing a very fast growing variety that is commonly stocked in inland lakes.

The rainbow was named for Meredith Gairdner, a prominent young naturalist employed by the Hudson Bay Company at Fort Vancouver.

Atlantic Salmon, *Salmo salar* Linnaeus

Scientific name: *Salmo* = from *salio,* meaning to leap (Latin); *salar* = a kind of trout (Latin).

As the object of one of the longest series of attempts to introduce a fish into Minnesota, the Atlantic salmon has been planted in this state since 1881 in habitats varying from North Shore streams to warm-water lakes. After a century, success may finally be at hand; in summer 1981 a 1-pound, 15-ounce, specimen was caught in the Sucker River, St. Louis County, and DNR personnel netted three males and one fertile female in Lake Superior off the mouth of the French River in the same county.

The Atlantic salmon is blue or brownish above and silvery below, with black spots dotting the body and often the dorsal and tail fins. In eastern North America, adults swim up streams to spawn and then either return to the ocean or die. The young stay for a year or two in the streams in which they hatched before they migrate downstream to the sea. Sea-run adults can exceed a weight of 60 pounds. The hook-and-line-record landlocked specimen is a 22½-pounder caught in Sebago Lake, Maine, in 1907.

In contrast to all of the Pacific salmons, the Atlantic salmon is known to survive after it spawns, with about 5 percent of those that spawn once living to do so again. The survivors are able to reverse the deterioration of the pituitary gland, adrenal glands, and kidneys associated in salmons with the stress of spawning migrations. Understanding how their bodies can rejuvenate themselves might have applications to human health, and scientists are studying the process.

Brown Trout, *Salmo trutta* Linnaeus

Scientific name: *Salmo* = from *Salio,* meaning to leap (Latin); *trutta* = trout (Latin).

The brown trout, another introduced species, is a native of European waters and was brought to the United States in 1883.

Brown trout. Photo by Dr. Don Beimborn.

The date of its introduction into Minnesota is uncertain, but it was probably in 1920.

The brown trout is olive green or brownish on its back and sides and yellowish white on its belly. Its sides are covered with rather large dark spots interspersed with large red or orange spots with pale margins. The spotting pattern varies. The dorsal fin is heavily spotted, but the tail fin has only a few spots confined to the dorsal lobe. The few spots on the tail fin and the absence of a crimson lateral band serve to distinguish the brown trout from the rainbow trout. The brown trout can be distinguished from the brook trout by the presence of dark spots, instead of light spots, on the sides and by the absence of wormlike streaks on the back. The coloration of older and larger brown trout may be more silvery and the dark spots on the sides may become reduced to small blotches, or X marks. Spawning males, especially stream residents, may become brightly colored, with reddish sides. Similar fish from lakes tend to be more silvery and the spotting may be obscured or it may form X marks.

Brown trout are autumn spawners. They construct nests in riffles similar to those of the rainbow trout and the brook trout. The young fish emerge from the gravel during the following spring. Occasionally, hybrids, known as tiger trout, between the brown and brook trout occur. Prof. Tom Waters showed the authors several hybrids from Valley Creek at Afton, Minnesota. Such hybrids are thought to be produced by the accidental fertilization of the eggs of either the brown trout or the brook trout

Tiger trout (hybrid of brook trout × brown trout). Photo by Dr. Don Beimborn.

by sperm produced by the opposite species. Since the two species are fall spawners and their nests may be adjacent to one another, chance fertilization is possible. It seems doubtful that there is actually direct mating between the two species; if there were, one would expect to find more hybrid tiger trout, assuming that hybrids have relatively high viability. A more careful study based on both field observations and controlled matings might answer the questions posed. Before the subject of hybridization is left, it should be pointed out that fish hybrids are more common than hybrids in any of the higher vertebrate groups, amphibians to mammals.

Brown trout in streams seldom weigh more than 12 pounds and generally average less than half that weight. Lake-dwelling fish may reach weights of more than 30 pounds and lengths of 3 feet or more. The world record for a hook-and-line brown trout is a 33-pound, 10-ounce, specimen caught in Flaming Gorge Lake, Utah, in 1977. The Minnesota record is 16 pounds, 8 ounces.

Brown trout are far more wary than brook trout, and it takes considerably more skill and patience to catch a brown trout than it does to catch a rainbow trout. The brown trout has been the salvation of fishery biologists managing trout streams, especially in urban settings, where there is tremendous fishing pressure. It would appear that the years of fishing selection in Europe prior to the brown trout's introduction into the United States plus the continued selection in the New World have produced a truly sophisticated and discriminating fish.

Round Whitefish, *Prosopium cylindraceum* (Pallas)

Scientific name: *Prosopium* = mask (Greek), referring to large bones in front of the eyes; *cylindraceum* = resembling a cylinder (Greek).

The round whitefish is a slender whitefish aptly named for its cylindrical shape. Members of the genus *Prosopium* have single flaps between the openings of their nostrils. Their snouts are sharper than that of the lake whitefish.

The round whitefish is distributed from Alaska and Canada eastward through the Great Lakes into northern New England. A similar species is found in Siberia. The round whitefish is present in Lake Superior but has never been very abundant. Round whitefish inhabit shallow inshore waters and do not range far out into the lake. They are an excellent food fish but were never an important commercial species.

Pygmy Whitefish, *Prosopium coulteri* (Eigenmann and Eigenmann)

Scientific name: *Prosopium* = mask (Greek), referring to large bones in front of the eyes; *coulteri* = named for J. M. Coulter, an early American explorer.

The pygmy whitefish is the smallest member of the whitefish group. It rarely reaches a length of 6 inches and is usually 3 or 4 inches long. Young pygmy whitefish have a row of dark vertical parr marks on their sides. The fish's small size and the number of scales in the lateral line series are characteristics that separate the pygmy whitefish from the round whitefish. The pygmy whitefish has fewer than 75 scales and the round whitefish more than 75 scales in the lateral series.

The distribution of this small whitefish is intriguing. It is found in the Pacific Northwest and in Lake Superior. In fact, its presence in Lake Superior was not discovered until 1953, when fishery biologists of the United States Fish and Wildlife Service took specimens while carrying out deep-water trawling. The pygmy whitefish lives in water 60 to 300 feet deep. The fish's small size and the large mesh of the gill nets used by commercial fishermen explain why the little fish were not collected; they simply swam through the large mesh. The pygmy whitefish must have had a much wider distribution throughout North America before and during the Pleistocene, or ice age; for some reason yet unknown, the species survived in eastern North America only in Lake Superior.

The pygmy whitefish is named for Dr. John Merle Coulter (1851–1928), a botanist and explorer in western North America.

Lake Whitefish, *Coregonus clupeaformis* (Mitchill)

Scientific name: *Coregonus* = angle eye (Greek); *clupeaformis* = herring shaped (Latin).

The lake whitefish is the largest whitefish in eastern North America. It is a deep-bodied fish with iridescent sides and a dark olive brown back. Its snout overhangs its lower jaw, and there are two small flaps between the openings of each nostril. The latter characteristic serves to distinguish members of the genus *Coregonus* from those belonging to the genus *Prosopium*, which have single flaps in the nostrils.

The lake whitefish is widely distributed throughout North America from Alaska and western Canada to the Atlantic coastal drainage of Maine and New Brunswick north to Labrador. The lake whitefish at one time was common throughout the Great Lakes, and it was once second in importance only to the lake trout in Lake Superior. However, its numbers have declined as a result of commercial fishing and the predation of the sea lamprey. Lake whitefish are cool-water fish and are found in a number of inland lakes in Minnesota, including Leech, Vermilion, Cass, Burntside, Snow Bank, the Red Lakes, Ten Mile, and Ball Club. Whitefish from these inland lakes reach a weight of 5 or 6 pounds, but the average is about 4 pounds. They are harvested in the autumn, October through November, with gill nets, and, later, after ice forms and thickens, they are taken with spears.

Mature lake whitefish come into shallow waters to spawn in the autumn and lay their eggs on shoals of gravel and rubble. The males develop small **tubercles** on their bodies and ventral fins that are called pearl organs. These tubercles give the body a rough, sandpaperlike texture. Spawning takes place at night, and the eggs are given no care. The eggs hatch in the following spring, and the larval and postlarval stages feed on plankton. When they reach a length of 3 or 4 inches, they switch to feeding on bottom-dwelling animals, such as snails, fingernail clams, and insect larvae. In some inland lakes, both the lake whitefish and the cisco leave the deep and cool waters in late June and July to feed on emerging mayflies and midges. At this time, both species can be caught on flies or small spinners; but, once the emergence, or hatch, is completed, they return to the deep and cool waters beneath the metalimnion (the zone where the temperature drops approximately 1° Celsius [C] per meter of depth). Therefore, lake whitefish are readily available to the angler only in the autumn and during the hatch of mayflies and midges.

Since declining in Lake Superior, the lake whitefish and the lake trout have been replaced by the smelt as commercial fishes. Today, most whitefishes available in the market or on menus come from the Canadian inland lake fisheries. Whitefishes are still extremely valuable and are fine and delicate tasting. They are excellent smoked or baked whole, cut into cubes in fish chowder and boiled, or broiled as filllets.

Dr. Samuel Latham Mitchill, pioneer American anthropologist, geologist, ornithologist, ichthyologist, zoologist, and walking encyclopedia on nature, first described the whitefish. In his *Fishes of New York*, published in 1815, he coined the trivial name *clupeaformis* for the lake whitefish, referring to its superficial similarity to the herring. Actually, it was the ciscoes and chubs that early Scandinavian fishermen in the Great Lakes referred to when they talked about herring. The generic name *Coregonus*, coined by Petrus Artedi and used by Linnaeus, is derived from Greek roots *kore*, pupil of the eye, and *gonia*, angle or corner, and was first applied to the European lavarent, or whitefish.

Cisco, *Coregonus artedi* LeSueur

Scientific name: *Coregonus* = angle eye (Greek);
artedi = named for Petrus Artedi, a Swedish naturalist.

The cisco, or lake herring, a species once very common in the Great Lakes, is now common only in Lake Superior. The Scan-

Dwarf cisco

dinavian immigrants who settled the shores of the Great Lakes and became commercial fishermen saw a similarity between the cisco and the herrings, family Clupeidae, which they had fished for in the Baltic and North Atlantic, and named these members of the salmon family lake herring. Overfishing, changes in the environment, introductions of other species of fishes (for example, the sea lamprey and the alewife), and other factors have all had an influence on the abundance of the cisco and its relatives in the Great Lakes.

A form of the cisco known as the tullibee is found in many of the lakes of northeastern and north-central Minnesota. The typical cisco is a slender, silvery fish, with an iridescent green back, that reaches a length of 14 inches and a weight of 3/4 pound. The inland tullibees may be deep bodied and attain a length of 20 inches and a weight of 5 pounds.

Ciscoes are cold-water fish, and they survive in lakes that are described as **oligotrophic,** that is, with few nutrients, or in those lakes in which oxygen is present below the metalimnion throughout the period of stratification. In the spring and autumn, ciscoes are found in the surface waters and shallows of the lake.

Ciscoes are autumn spawners, breeding just before or at the time of ice formation. At that time, large schools of mature fish enter the shallows and spawn, usually at night. In autumn they can be taken with gill nets set in 6 to 9 feet of water. Usually, each lake has its own special dates when netting is permitted;

the dates are set by Minnesota DNR fishery personnel. There are restrictions on the size of mesh and the length of net that may be used. Contrary to the belief of many anglers, gill nets do not take walleyes but may take an occasional large northern pike. The northern pike are preying on the ciscoes in the shallow water and may attempt to catch a cisco struggling in the net and thus become captured, too. The northern pike are not harmed and can be released none the worse and apparently none the wiser for their experience when the net is lifted. Northern pike tend to roll the net and reduce its efficiency; they also cover the webbing with viscous mucous secretions.

Ciscoes can be caught on a hook and line in the winter and the early summer before the lakes become stratified. They can also be caught in the summer with small worms fished below the metalimnion, but there are few people who fish for ciscoes. In the winter, people icefishing take them by using yellow or white grubs, the larva of the goldenrod gallfly. In the spring, ciscoes can be taken on flies or small spinners. Ciscoes are an underused, high-quality food fish that could provide considerable sporting potential in northern waters.

Ciscoes are generally referred to as whitefish and so can be confused with the lake whitefish. The cisco has a terminal mouth, or its lower jaw may protrude. The lake whitefish has an overhanging snout and upper jaw. Many so-called smoked whitefish are actually smoked ciscoes, but there is little, if any, difference in the delightful quality of the flesh. Ciscoes and lake whitefish serve as intermediate hosts for the tapeworm *Trianophorus* and at times may be wormy. The larval worms develop into adult tapeworms in the northern pike, but they are not harmful to humans. Of course, all fish should be well cooked, smoked, or pickled before it is eaten. In addition, ciscoes can be broiled, baked, or used in a delicious fish chowder.

Ciscoes feed on microscopic crustaceans that compose the animal portion of the plankton, principally various species of cladocerans. Occasionally, ciscoes may feed on the larvae of insects and on emerging midges, mayflies, and caddisflies. When a major emergence of insects occurs in late spring, the entire surface of a lake inhabited by ciscoes may be covered with dimples of feeding fish. It is at this time that great sport can be had with a fly rod.

In some lakes in Minnesota where the cisco and lake whitefish occur together (such as Burntside, Snowbank, and Ten Mile), the cisco is slim and dwarfed, reaching a maximum length of 6 inches. Dwarf ciscoes released into other lakes where the whitefish is absent start growing normally, a suggestion that competition from the lake whitefish can inhibit growth in ciscoes.

The cisco is of historical interest because it has as a trivial name *artedi*, after Petrus Artedi, the father of ichthyology. Carl Linnaeus, the founder of our system of naming animals and plants (the system of nomenclature), and Artedi were colleagues in 1728 at the College of Medicine, Uppsala, Sweden. Both young scholars were interested in botany and zoology and in devising a system of classification for plants and animals. They made a pact providing that, if either should die, the survivor would carry on the observations of the other. Eight years later, while visiting Linnaeus in Holland, Artedi fell into a canal and was drowned. Linnaeus wrote, "Thus did the most distinguished of ichthyologists perish in the waters having devoted his life to the discovery of their inhabitants" (Wilfred Blunt, 1971, *The Compleat Naturalist: A Life of Linnaeus*, New York: Viking Press). Linnaeus continued their joint work and named a genus of plants *Artedia* in his colleague's memory. LeSueur honored the earlier contributions of Artedi by naming the cisco after him in a paper read March 3, 1818, to the Philadelphia Academy of Natural Sciences.

Shortjaw Cisco, *Coregonus zenithicus* (Jordan and Evermann)

Scientific name: *Coregonus* = angle eye (Greek); *zenithicus* = derived from the name applied to Duluth, Minnesota, as the Zenith City.

The shortjaw cisco is a slender fish with a bluish green back, silvery sides, and a whitish belly. The scales have pigmentation around the free margins. The length of the lower jaw is equal to, or just slightly shorter than, that of the upper jaw. The gill rakers are relatively shorter, shorter than those of *C. artedi*. The shortjaw cisco has fewer gill rakers on the first gill arch (usually fewer than 42) than *C. artedi* (43 or more).

The shortjaw cisco was known originally from lakes Michigan, Huron, Superior, and Nipigon. Today, it is known only from Lake Superior and Lake Nipigon. Its disappearance from the other Great Lakes is probably due to overfishing. The shortjaw cisco lives in waters 60 to 600 feet deep but is more at home at less than 200 feet and close to shore.

Bloater, *Coregonus hoyi* (Gill)

Scientific name: *Coregonus* = angle eye (Greek); *hoyi* = named for H. R. Hoy, an American naturalist.

The bloater is a small, deep-water cisco that rarely exceeds 8 inches in length. The body is silverish, with an iridescent back. Its mandible has a tubercle on the tip and is pigmented.

The bloater is found in all the Great Lakes except Lake Erie, but it has declined drastically in Lake Ontario. The species is abundant in Lake Superior and is found from inshore areas to 20 miles out in the lake and from depths of 150 to 600 feet. Bloaters have little value as a sport or a commercial fish because of their small size.

The bloater is named for Dr. Hilo R. Hoy, an able naturalist from Racine, Wisconsin, who was one of the very early collectors of Lake Michigan fishes.

Kiyi, *Coregonus kiyi* (Koelz)

Scientific name: *Coregonus* = angle eye (Greek); *kiyi* = Lake Michigan commercial fishermen's name for this species.

The kiyi, like the bloater, a small, deep-water whitefish that reaches a length of 6 to 8 inches. The body coloration in the two is similar. The kiyi has a thinner mandible and a more prominent knob at the tip of the lower jaw than the bloater. The most useful characteristic for distinguishing the two species is the number of rakers on the first gill arch. The kiyi has fewer than 38 rakers and the bloater has more than 38.

The kiyi once had a distribution throughout the Great Lakes except Lake Erie. Over the years, the numbers of kiyi have declined, and it now survives only in Lake Superior (Thomas

Todd, personal communication). It appears that the kiyi has declined in numbers in Lake Superior as well and may be on its way to extinction, along with several other species of whitefishes once common to the Great Lakes.

Family OSMERIDAE
The Smelts

The family Osmeridae is a marine family that contains 10 species of small, slender fishes. Some live in estuaries and others are anadromous, entering rivers and streams to spawn. Only one species, the rainbow smelt, *Osmerus mordax*, is found in the Great Lakes, including Lake Superior.

Rainbow Smelt, *Osmerus mordax* (Mitchill)

Scientific name: *Osmerus* = from *osme*, meaning odor (Greek); *mordax* = biting (Latin).

The rainbow smelt is a small, slender fish that can reach a length of 15 inches after four years of life. The rainbow smelt was introduced into five lakes in Michigan in 1912 as food for

Rainbow smelt

landlocked salmon planted in that state. It escaped into Lake Michigan and spread throughout the Great Lakes except Lake Ontario (to which it is native). Its presence in the Minnesota waters of Lake Superior was verified in 1946. Since that time, its populations have increased tremendously, and each spring tens to hundreds of thousands migrate up the tributary streams on the North Shore to spawn. This annual event is an occasion for a fishing phenomenon known as smelting. Thousands of Minnesotans from all over the state and residents of the other Lake States rush to the streams when the call is put out that "the smelt are running." Local radio stations, television announcers, newspapers, and DNR information hot lines keep the public informed of the impending run, a harbinger of spring. Local groups that harvest smelt freeze some and use others for the familiar smelt fries of various church and veterans' groups.

Dip nets, seines, and all manner of gear are used to harvest this small, silvery fish. Night is the preferred time for the spawning migration, but during peak runs the smelt may surge into the streams both day and night. The spawning activity is usually completed within a week or 10 days. The surviving adults return to the lake to continue their predaceous existence. The eggs hatch rapidly, and the larval smelt drift downstream into the lake, where they feed at first on tiny animals in the plankton. By the end of their first year of life, they have begun feeding on small fishes.

Unfortunately, smelt have been introduced into several Minnesota lakes by well-meaning fishing enthusiasts to provide food for lake trout and other large, predaceous game fishes. Smelt are now present in at least one boundary-waters lake and have or soon may migrate throughout the lake region of the Hudson Bay drainage system. What impact this very prolific and voracious predator may have on the native fish fauna of these relatively unproductive and fragile lakes, one cannot know. When feeding on plankton, the young smelt may compete with the plankton-feeding larval walleyes and lake trout and hence reduce the potential production of these very valuable sport fishes. In fact, because the growth rates of game fishes tend to be low in the border lakes, the competition may continue for several years. The argument might be presented that the smelt may provide potential food for the large walleyes and lake trout. This may well be true, but the balance sheet may still end with red ink because the losses of young walleyes and lake trout may exceed the gains in numbers of large fishes.

There seems to be little hope that the spread of the smelt throughout the boundary waters can be controlled. The mature female can lay 12,000 to 50,000 eggs, so only a few fish could colonize a whole lake. The smelt's successful colonization of the Great Lakes, especially Lake Superior, indicates its adaptability to new habitats. Fortunately, fishery biologists are aware of the introduction and can continue to monitor the changes that take place and the time it takes for the smelt to migrate throughout the drainage.

Smelt resemble ciscoes and whitefishes but differ in their having strong teeth on their jaws, larger scales, and no pelvic axillary processes.

The generic name *Osmerus* is another name coined by Artedi. It is derived from the Greek word meaning odorous and is equivalent to the Anglo-Saxon English word for smelt.

Family CYPRINIDAE
The Minnows

Minnows are usually small, but some, such as the introduced grass carp and other species native to the western United States, may reach a weight of 20 to 100 pounds. There are more than 300 species of minnows known from North and Central America, and the minnow family contains more species than any other family of fish native to the fresh waters of the North American continent. In Minnesota, there are 41 native species of minnows, plus 3 that have been introduced from Europe or Asia. They represent almost one-third of the fish fauna of the state and clearly outnumber the species of any other family. It is possible that, in terms of total numbers of individuals, minnows may number in the hundreds of millions, if not in the billions.

Minnows occupy a wide variety of habitats and feed on a wide variety of organisms. Most species require a relatively short period of time, two or three years, to reach sexual maturity and produce many eggs. Minnows are generally small, and so a large number can occupy a small space and still find sufficient food and shelter. All of these characteristics and factors serve to explain the large numbers of individuals that exist.

Not all small fishes are minnows; many are the young of other fishes. A number of characteristics serve to separate other small fishes from true minnows. All minnows have naked heads except during the breeding season, when mature males may develop tubercles. Some minnows also develop bright colors during breeding season, as suggested by such names as redside dace, redbelly dace, rosyface shiner, red shiner, and redfin shiner. A single dorsal fin with fewer than 10 soft rays is characteristic of all native minnows. In the introduced carp and goldfish, the dorsal fin has a hard ray and more than 10 soft rays. Minnows lack teeth on their jaws but have specialized teeth in their throat (pharynx) regions (Figure 41). These **pharyngeal teeth** are useful in identifying the various minnow species.

Minnows are an important food resource for larger fishes and represent an essential link in the aquatic food chain leading to the game species such as the walleye, northern pike, and basses. Minnows are also of direct economic value to the bait industry.

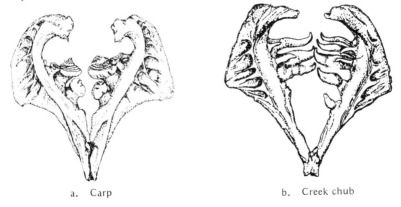

a. Carp   b. Creek chub

Figure 41. Pharyngeal teeth of (a) the carp and (b) the creek chub.

Carp

Carp, *Cyprinus carpio* Linnaeus

Scientific name: *Cyprinus* = early Greek name for carp; *carpio* = carp (Latin).

The carp is a large minnow that is native to Asia. It has been widely introduced throughout the world as a game fish and as a commercial food fish. The carp and the goldfish are really domestic fishes, both having been bred and reared for thousands of years in the Orient. The carp was raised primarily for food and the goldfish as pets and for ornamental display.

The carp is brassy to olive green in color. The dorsal fin is long and has more than 10 soft rays. Both the dorsal and anal fins have a hard ray. Two pairs of barbels are present at the angle of the upper jaw.

Carp were first introduced into California in 1872, and in 1877 the United States Fish Commission stocked carp in some experimental ponds in Washington, D.C. The stocking of Minnesota waters took place in 1883. Today, the carp is abundant in southern Minnesota, where anglers consider it a trash fish. Commercial fishermen harvest it in abundance and market it mostly in other states. Large amounts of money are spent to control the growth of existing populations and their spread into carp-free lakes. Initially, however, the carp was difficult to get established. In fact, it was protected by law from exploitation. What a difference a century makes. Today, there are penalties for transplanting carp or using live carp for bait.

Three varieties of carp exist in North America: the scale carp, the mirror carp, and the leather carp. The latter variety lacks scales, and the scaleless skin has the appearance of tanned leather. The mirror carp has only a few large scales on its body. The scaled variety is the common carp. European and Asian fishery biologists have developed by selective breeding a number of different genetic strains of carp. Their selection experiments have produced strains that have desirable characteristics, such as rapid growth, high protein content, and high efficiency in converting fish food to fish protein. These strains of carp are comparable to the breeds of milk and beef cattle, sheep, and pigs that are familiar to North Americans. The carp strains are similar to chickens as far as efficiency of feed conversion is concerned; the amount of protein produced per unit of intake is very high.

Goldfish, *Carassius auratus* (Linnaeus)

Scientific name: *Carassius* = Medieval Latin word for carp; *auratus* = gilded (Latin).

The goldfish is probably familiar to more people than any other species of fish, but these people may not be aware that the goldfish has been introduced into the wild in many parts of North America, including Minnesota. The goldfish has been domesticated in its native range of China and Japan. Goldfish can be distinguished from native minnows by the presence of a strong, hard ray in the dorsal and anal fins and by its having more than 10 soft rays in the dorsal fin. The goldfish may resemble a small carp superficially, but it can be easily distinguished

Goldfish

by the absence of barbels on its upper jaw. Wild goldfish are olive green or blackish in color.

The goldfish is known from several lakes in St. Paul and Minneapolis, including Lake Calhoun, Como Lake, and Silver Lake. Occasionally, goldfish are reported from central and southern Minnesota lakes, but they are apparently less adaptable than the carp and have failed to become established there. There is a thriving population in the Shellrock River near Albert Lea, Minnesota. These wild populations probably originated with parolees from the fishbowls of vacationing families or escapees from ornamental fish ponds. In the eastern part of the United States, goldfish have become a management problem comparable to the carp in the Midwest. Goldfish can reach a length of more than 12 inches and a weight of more than 2 pounds — they are by no means small fish.

The goldfish has been bred for hundreds of generations in Asia, and there are as many breeds, or varieties, of goldfish as there are breeds of cats and dogs combined. Individual fish of certain breeds may be valued in excess of $10,000, and they are as highly prized by their owners as fine horses, cats, and dogs. In the orient, showings of goldfish are as common as pet shows are in the United States. To all but their owners and other goldfish fanciers, the breeds are grotesque; some goldfish have large, bulging eyes; some, large, protruding foreheads; and others, large, fanlike tails or multiple fins. Their beauty is truly in the eye of the beholders, their owners.

Grass Carp, *Ctenopharyngodon idella* (Valenciennes)

Scientific name: *Ctenopharyngodon* = comblike throat teeth (Greek); *idella* = distinct (Greek).

The grass carp, or white amur, is a close relative of the carp. It was first brought to the United States in 1963, when it was introduced into Arkansas. It is a large minnow said to reach a weight of 100 pounds in its native Asia. It is olive brown on the back and silvery white below. The scales on the back are dark at their edges in a way similar to those of the carp. The grass carp can be distinguished from the carp by its relatively large mouth and by its dorsal fin, which lacks a hard ray and has only 8 rays to the carp's 17 to 21.

Since its introduction, the grass carp has entered the Mississippi River system and is spreading northward. Several specimens have been captured in the Mississippi and Missouri rivers, including a 21-pound individual from the Mississippi near Chester, Illinois, in 1971.

The grass carp is a strong swimmer that is difficult to net or trap. Although versatile in diet, it feeds mostly on aquatic vegetation and was imported to control water plants in artificial impoundments. It has a voracious appetite and can consume the equivalent of its own weight in food each day. It does not digest all it eats, however, and passes considerable quantities of partly digested plant matter back into the water. In doing so, it provides nutrients that stimulate the growth of algae.

Only time will reveal the full results of the release of the grass carp in this country. However, the size it attains, its adaptability, and its behavior suggest that it could possibly become a nuisance that rivals the carp. In Minnesota, this fish might have the added disadvantage of occupying habitats that the European carp uses relatively lightly, that is, swift, warm-water streams, such as the upper St. Croix and Snake rivers. It seems especially ironic that this fish was released in this country after the lesson taught by the carp.

The grass carp has not been reported from the Mississippi itself in Minnesota, but it has been taken from a pond close to the river near Winona. In July 1977, a new property owner noticed unusual fish in a pond that overflows into Gilmore Creek, which in turn flows into Lake Winona. A biologist from Winona State University speared two of these fish and shot another with an arrow. He identified all three as grass carp. On July 11, the property owner reported the identifications to the Minnesota DNR. Between July 11 and July 27, DNR personnel removed 12 more grass carp, all that remained in the pond. Each of these fish weighed about 6 pounds.

Officials of the DNR are already concerned that the grass carp might destroy wild rice beds and disturb aquatic vegetation to the detriment of native fishes, waterfowl, and furbearers, and they are making every effort to keep the grass carp out of Minnesota. Anyone knowing of this fish in Minnesota should inform the DNR immediately.

Blacknose dace

Blacknose Dace, *Rhinichthys atratulus* (Hermann)

Scientific name: *Rhinichthys* = snout fish (Greek); *atratulus* = probably from *atratus* (Greek), meaning wearing black, as for mourning.

The blacknose dace reaches a length of about 3½ inches. The upper part of its body is dark brown to brownish black and is spotted with numerous black blotches; the lower part of its body is silvery, with a sprinkling of small dark spots. The upper lip is connected directly to the snout and is not separated by a groove (the groove is characteristic of many minnows). A small barbel is present at the end of the upper jaw in the corner of the mouth. In May and early June, breeding males develop a dusky red lateral band.

Male and female blacknose dace construct nests of small pebbles in riffles during June and early July. No care is provided for the eggs nor for the young that hatch.

The blacknose dace is widely distributed in North America in rivers and streams from Manitoba and North Dakota to Nova Scotia and southward as far as North Carolina and Nebraska.

Longnose Dace, *Rhinichthys cataractae* (Valenciennes)

Scientific name: *Rhinichthys* = snout fish (Greek); *cataractae* = of the cataract (Greek).

The longnose dace is usually small, 2 or 3 inches long, but occasionally an individual can reach a length of 6 inches. The

Longnose dace

longnose dace resembles the blacknose dace but has a much more elongated snout that extends far beyond the end of the upper jaw. Small longnose dace are evenly pigmented and usually soft brown in color, but they become brownish black as they grow. They lack the blotching that is characteristic of the blacknose dace. Breeding male longnose dace develop brownish red bands on their sides.

Longnose dace are widely distributed throughout North America from northwestern Canada eastward through the Great Lakes and the eastern United States. The longnose dace lives in very rapid waters, cataracts, where it seems almost impossible that any fish could exist without being swept away by the current. Close observation reveals that this dace is living on the bottom, on the margins of large rocks and boulders, and that it is actually away from the full force of the current. When the dace is disturbed, it may be carried downstream by the velocity of the water, but it quickly swims to the bottom where the velocity is reduced and then darts into a crevice between rocks. The **swim bladder** of the longnose dace is reduced in size compared to other minnows, which reduces the bouyancy of the fish and enables it to remain on the bottom more easily. The longnose dace and the blacknose dace are found together, but the latter species lives in quieter waters near the feet of rapids. In large lakes, such as Lake of the Woods, Mille Lacs, Lake Superior, and Leech, the longnose dace may live along the rocky shoreline, where the waves pounding on the beach create a habitat similar to that of a swift stream. It is commonly found in trout streams.

Lake Chub, *Couesius plumbeus* (Agassiz)

Scientific name: *Couesius* = named for Eliot Coues, an American ornithologist; *plumbeus* = lead colored (Latin).

The lake chub can reach a length of 5 inches. Its body is long and stout, dark olive above and gradually merging with dusky white below. Its small mouth is terminal. It has a slender barbel near the posterior tip of its lower jaw. Breeding males are tinged with reddish orange on the sides, posterior to the head.

The lake chub is distributed throughout northern North America from the Yukon and Fraser rivers eastward through Canada to Nova Scotia. It is present in the Lake Superior drainage westward through the boundary waters to the Lake of the Woods drainage. Populations of the lake chub occur in the upper Missouri drainage of Wyoming, South Dakota, and the Sand Hills of Nebraska. Isolated, presumably relict populations are also known from eastern Iowa.

The generic name *Couesius* commemorates the contributions of the eminent ornithologist Eliot Coues, of the United States Army Medical Corps.

Hornyhead Chub, *Nocomis biguttatus* (Kirtland)

Scientific name: *Nocomis* = Indian name applied by Girard to this genus; *biguttatus* = two spotted (Latin).

The hornyhead chub is one of Minnesota's larger native minnows. It reaches a length of nearly 12 inches. This chub has a distinct barbel on the posterior tip of the jaw. A dark lateral band extends from the eye to the base of the tail fin and terminates in a prominent black spot. The body is dark olive brown above the band and silvery or a dusky silver below.

In the spring, mature males develop numerous spiny tubercles on their heads. These hornlike tubercles give the chub its common name, hornyhead. Males also have a prominent red spot posterior to the eyes and reddish orange pigment on the fins. Females are more drab and do not develop tubercles. In early May, the males begin the construction of nests, small de-

Hornyhead chub

pressions or piles of small stones, in the riffles of small- to medium-size streams. Females then join the males and egg laying begins. Fertilization is external, and the fertilized eggs fall into the crevices between the pebbles and stones forming the nest. The males then add more pebbles to the nests, spawning continues with other females, and eventually the nests may reach a diameter of 3 feet and a depth of 6 inches. When spawning is completed, the males desert the nests. In a week to 10 days, the eggs hatch. Other species of minnows may then appropriate the nest sites or the pebbles and stones accumulated by the late tenants. In fact, in May and June the same riffle may be used in succession by more than a dozen different species.

The hornyhead chub is found in streams from Wyoming and the Dakotas eastward through the Great Lakes to the Hudson River and southward through the Ohio River basin to Oklahoma. It is rare in lakes but may be taken in such habitats near the mouths of small- and medium-size streams.

These chubs bite on baited hooks and will take artificial flies and small spinners. They are often the quarry of children at the old swimming hole.

Silver Chub, *Hybopsis storeriana* (Kirtland)

Scientific name: *Hybopsis* = rounded face (Greek); *storeriana* = named for D. H. Storer, an American ichthyologist.

The silver chub reaches a maximum length of 10 inches. It is a silvery minnow with a light dusky lateral band and a greenish

Silver chub

iridescent back. Its snout protrudes beyond its mouth. A long and slender barbel is present at the posterior tip of its upper jaw. The origin of the dorsal fin is in front of the origin of the pelvic fins.

The silver chub is a large-river species and inhabits the Red River, Minnesota River, the Mississippi River below St. Anthony Falls, and the St. Croix River below Taylors Falls. It is common in river lakes, such as Lake St. Croix and Lake Pepin. The silver chub ranges from eastern North Dakota east to New York and south to Alabama and Oklahoma.

Gravel Chub, *Hybopsis x-punctata* Hubbs and Crowe

Scientific name: *Hybopsis* = rounded face (Greek); *x-punctata* = from *punctatus*, meaning spotted (Latin), referring to the shape of the spots on the sides.

The gravel chub is usually less than 4 inches in total length. Its body is a pale silver to light straw color, with a very faint lateral stripe. The most striking feature of this chub is the X-shaped spots on the sides of its body. These spots give this attractive little fish its trivial name, *x-punctata*. As do other members of the genus *Hybopsis*, the gravel chub has a slender barbel at the posterior tip of its upper jaw.

The gravel chub is known from the extreme southeastern corner of Minnesota. It has been collected from the Root and upper Iowa rivers. From Minnesota it ranges eastward to Ohio and southward to Arkansas and Oklahoma.

Speckled chub

Speckled Chub, *Hybopsis aestivalis* (Girard)

Scientific name: *Hybopsis* = rounded face (Greek); *aestivalis* = summer (Latin).

The speckled chub is a slender minnow that reaches a length of about 2½ inches. The body is a pale silver and speckled with small, black pigment spots above the lateral line. A very prominent barbel is present at the posterior tip of the upper jaw. The snout is blunt and protrudes over the mouth.

The habitat of the speckled chub is a shifting sandy bottom in medium to large rivers, such as the Minnesota, Mississippi, St. Croix, Cannon, and Zumbro rivers. This little fish when alive is almost translucent, and it can easily be overlooked in a seine unless it wiggles. It ranges from the Missouri River drainage in Iowa northeastward through southern Minnesota and southward to western Florida and the Rio Grande.

Creek Chub, *Semotilus atromaculatus* (Mitchill)

Scientific name: *Semotilus* = from *sema*, meaning banner (Greek), referring to the dorsal fin, with the second part used by its author to mean spotted; *atromaculatus* = black spot (Latin).

The creek chub, one of Minnesota's larger native minnows, reaches a length of more than 12 inches. The body of this chub is dusky silver, with a dark brownish black back and a pronounced lateral black band that terminates in a diffuse black spot at the base of the tail fin. The dorsal fin has a prominent black spot at

Creek chub

its anterior base, located on the membranes between the first and third rays. A small barbel may be present in a groove a short distance in front of the posterior tip of the upper jaw, but specimens from the upper Mississippi River may lack this barbel on one side or both sides of their mouths.

The creek chub is an inhabitant of small- and medium-size rivers, and only occasionally is it found in lakes or large rivers. The species is found from Montana eastward to the Canadian Atlantic provinces and southward to the Gulf of Mexico. Creek chubs are occasionally used as bait but are not as popular with anglers as many other minnow species are. They bit readily on flies and spinners, and anglers looking for trout recognize them as great bait stealers. Large creek chubs are quite tasty and have a sweet taste according to old-timers. Unfortunately, in Minnesota fishing for minnows is the sport of small children, despite the influence of Old World anglers who seek out various species, such as loaches and bream, as game fishes.

The generic name *Semotilus*, coined by the great Rafinesque, refers to the creek chub's spotted dorsal fin. Dr. Mitchill, in his description of the species, used *atromaculatus* to refer again to the prominent black spot.

Pearl Dace, *Semotilus margarita* (Cope)

Scientific name: *Semotilus* = from *sema*, meaning banner (Greek), referring to the dorsal fin, with the second part used by its author to mean spotted; *margarita* = pearl (Greek).

The pearl dace is a medium-size minnow, usually not more than 5 inches in total length, with small scales and a mottled appearance. Young pearl dace resemble creek chubs, and the two species can be confused. The pearl dace lacks the pigment spot in the dorsal fin characteristic of the creek chub, and the dace has a smaller mouth.

The pearl dace occurs in lakes and streams from northwestern Canada through the northern United States, from the Rockies to the eastern Great Lakes, and from Vermont south to Virginia east of the Allegheny Mountains.

Prof. Ulysses O. Cox of the Mankato Normal School carried out the first survey of the fishes of Minnesota in the last decade of the nineteenth century. The survey was carried out under the direction of Prof. Henry Nachtrieb, a member of the Department of Animal Biology, University of Minnesota, and director of the Minnesota Zoological Survey. During the survey of Mille Lacs, Cox found a minnow that he thought was new to science, and he named it *Semotilus nachtriebi* as an expression of his high esteem for Nachtrieb. Subsequently, a thorough study of all the species in the genus *Semotilus* revealed that Cox's fish was simply a geographic race of *S. margarita*. Today, specimens of the pearl dace from Mille Lacs, southeastern Minnesota, and the remainder of the state are known by the trinomial, or subspecific, name *S. margarita nachtriebi* (Cox).

Redside Dace, *Clinostomus elongatus* (Kirtland)

Scientific name: *Clinostomus* = inclined mouth (Greek); *elongatus* = elongate (Latin).

The redside dace reaches a maximum length of about 5 inches. Its snout is very sharp and its mouth is large; its lower jaw is projecting. The redside dace's body is steel blue, mottled with dusky silver on its belly. There is a light band on the body between the dark lateral band and the steel blue color of the back. Breeding males have a bright reddish orange band of rectangular shape on the sides of their bodies between the pectoral and pelvic fins. The breeding females are reddish brown. Both sexes have small pearl organs, or tubercles, over most of their bodies.

The redside dace ranges from southeastern Minnesota through part of the eastern Great Lakes and the Ohio River drainage to northeastern Oklahoma. In Minnesota, it is found in the small headwater streams of the Cannon, Zumbro, and Root rivers. It appears to have been quite sensitive to habitat modifications throughout its native range, and it survives in streams where intensive agriculture is difficult, such as small headwater streams where bedrock is near or at the surface.

Southern Redbelly Dace, *Phoxinus erythrogaster* (Rafinesque)

Scientific name: *Phoxinus* = a Greek name for some kind of fish; *erythrogaster* = red belly (Greek).

The southern redbelly dace and its close relative, the northern redbelly dace, are the most beautiful of Minnesota's minnows.

Southern redbelly dace showing red breeding color

From spring through summer, adults are colored brilliantly with crimson on the belly and yellow on the fins, sides, and **caudal peduncle.** The bright colors might help breeding adults recognize each other on the spawning beds that they share with other small fishes. Female southern redbelly dace reach a length of about 4 inches, males about 3 inches.

The distribution of the southern redbelly dace is centered in the Ozarks and extends into southern Minnesota in the lower Mississippi River system. This dace is known in Minnesota as far north as tributaries of the Cannon River in Goodhue County. Small, clear headwater streams form the habitat preferred by the southern redbelly dace throughout its range. It lives in various stream gradients and over various bottom types — sand, gravel, and mud — but consistently lives where springs are present. Its abundance in small streams in Minnesota in warm months contrasts its apparent scarcity in them in the winter. It seems to migrate downstream toward large streams and rivers as winter approaches.

Isolated populations of the southern redbelly dace are known from clear streams in Kansas, Mississippi, New Mexico, and Oklahoma. The existence of these populations suggests that this dace was formerly more widely distributed than it is now and that habitat destruction has eliminated it from all but the most pristine places. In fact, the recent cutting of trees along the stream in Mississippi in which this dace lived, with the resulting loss of shade, may have eliminated that population.

The southern redbelly dace and the northern redbelly dace resemble each other closely, and small individuals of the two species are virtually indistinguishable. Both species are dark brown on top and creamy on the bottom when they are not in breeding dress. Both have two blackish stripes on each side. The upper stripe especially is broken into dots. The southern redbelly dace grows larger than the northern redbelly dace, and adults can be distinguished by the shape of their heads. In small individuals (less than an inch long) of both species, the snout is short and the mouth upturned. The northern redbelly dace stays this way for life, but, as the southern redbelly dace grows, its snout becomes longer and its mouth becomes more horizontal (Figure 42a).

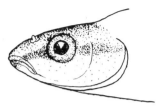 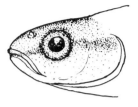

a. Southern redbelly dace   b. Northern redbelly dace

Figure 42. Heads of (a) the southern redbelly dace and (b) the northern redbelly dace.

A small minnow with a small mouth and a long intestine the length of which helps digest plant matter, the southern redbelly dace eats mostly tiny water plants that it grazes from rocks and the substrate. Various kinds of algae, chiefly diatoms, are known to form most of its diet in certain streams in southern Minnesota. It also eats small animals, such as water fleas and insects, when given the opportunity.

The flashing bodies of southern redbelly dace present a colorful scene in spring on the gravelly spawning grounds of small streams. From one to four males chase receptive females and attempt to pin them to the substrate. Breeding fish develop small tubercles on their pectoral fins and scales. These tubercles are better developed in males. They are used in combat and to help hold females when spawning. Spawning is accomplished either by one female and one male or by a threesome of one female and two males. The males hold the female between them and vibrate their bodies, apparently stimulating the female to shed eggs. The eggs are scattered among pebbles on the bottom and are left unattended. Hybrids are known of the southern redbelly dace and other kinds of minnows that use the same spawning grounds, such as the common shiner, creek chub, Ozark minnow, redside dace, and stoneroller.

Northern Redbelly Dace, *Phoxinus eos* (Cope)

Scientific name: *Phoxinus* = a Greek name for some kind of fish; *eos* = dawn (Greek).

As its name suggests, the northern redbelly dace is generally found in regions north of where the southern redbelly dace is found; it occurs from the Northwest Territories and western and eastern Canada through the northern and eastern United States. It lives in streams, bogs, and lakes, often in quiet places over a silty bottom. It may live in acid bogs, where the water is colored brown. Known from all drainage basins in Minnesota, it is most common in the northern half of the state.

In coloration the northern redbelly dace closely resembles the southern redbelly dace. The northern redbelly dace is smaller, however, seldom exceeding a length of 3 inches, and its snout remains short and blunt throughout its life (Figure 42b).

The northern redbelly dace eats algae and tiny aquatic animals. It spawns in the early summer in Minnesota, when it acquires crimson and yellow colors. Its breeding tubercles are less developed than those of the southern redbelly dace. Spawning females are attended by one or more males. Spawning behavior similar to that of the southern redbelly dace has been observed over gravelly riffles in Colorado streams. In artificial ponds, spawning and deposition of eggs have been noted to occur in masses of filamentous algae.

Hybrids between the northern redbelly dace and the southern redbelly dace have not been reported, and hybrids would be difficult to recognize even if they did occur. The northern redbelly dace does, however, hybridize commonly with the finescale dace, *Phoxinus neogaeus,* a fish it resembles less closely than it does the southern redbelly dace. Remarkably, hybrids of the northern redbelly dace and the finescale dace seem more abundant in certain places, including some bogs in northern Minnesota, than either parent species. Furthermore, it has been shown that female hybrids (the only sex known in hybrids) are fertile and can breed with males of both the northern redbelly dace and the finescale dace. These two distinct species are, therefore, sufficiently similar in genetic composition to breed and produce offspring that are normal in the sense that they are fertile, a highly unusual situation.

Northern redbelly dace showing red breeding color

Finescale dace showing yellow breeding color

Finescale Dace, *Phoxinus neogaeus* Cope

Scientific name: *Phoxinus* = a Greek name for some kind of fish; *neogaeus* = new world (Greek).

A northern species, the finescale dace has two main population centers, one from the Northwest Territories to southern Alberta and one from the Hudson Bay drainage through eastern Canada, the Great Lakes region, and the eastern United States. Isolated populations are known from Colorado, Nebraska, South Dakota, and Wyoming. This dace lives in lakes, streams, and ponds. It is most common in Minnesota in bogs in the northern reaches of the state, where it often occurs with the brook stickleback, the northern redbelly dace, and the pearl dace.

The finescale dace is larger and more carnivorous than its close relatives, the redbelly dace. It reaches a length of about 5 inches. It is brown on top and whitish on the bottom, with greenish sides, each of which bears one lateral stripe. Crimson and yellow coloration develop on the lower body of breeding adults, most intensely in males.

In comparison to the redbelly dace, the finescale dace has a large mouth and a short intestine. It eats algae when young and continues to eat small plants throughout its life but adds small animals to its diet as it grows. Typically, insects are a part of its diet, and tiny clams are known to be a common food in northern Minnesota. This dace is a hardy fish sold as bait in Minnesota and Canada.

In April and May, just after the ice is off the bogs and streams of northern Minnesota, the finescale dace starts spawning. The bright breeding colors develop and the rays of the pectoral fins of males become swollen, evidently to serve some function in spawning. The spawning act, however, has not been observed. Hybridization with the northern redbelly dace takes place freely, and little genetic difference separates the two species even though they are distinct from each other in appearance.

Suckermouth Minnow, *Phenacobius mirabilis* (Girard)

Scientific name: *Phenacobius* = impostor (Greek), referring to the suckerlike appearance of this species; *mirabilis* = wonderful (Latin).

The suckermouth minnow reaches a length of 4 inches. As its common name implies, it has a suckerlike mouth. Its upper lip is fleshy, but its lower lip has only fleshy lobes and is not entirely fleshy as in the true suckers. Its cylindrical body is iridescent olive green above a prominent lateral band, about the width of the eye, that extends from the tip of the snout to a spot at the base of the tail fin. The lower part of its body is dusky silver.

The suckermouth minnow ranges from eastern Colorado and South Dakota to western Ohio, south to Louisiana and Texas. It is rare in Minnesota, restricted to the streams tributary to the Mississippi River south of Hastings.

Golden Shiner, *Notemigonus crysoleucas* (Mitchill)

Scientific name: *Notemigonus* = angled back (Greek); *crysoleucas* = golden white (Greek).

The golden shiner is a deep-bodied minnow that reaches a length of more than 8 inches. The body has a rich gold tinge when the minnow is alive, but this color fades rapidly when the

Golden shiner

fish is removed from the water. Its body is compressed, and the lateral line is decurved.

Golden shiners seem to prefer lakes, but young individuals are found occasionally in rivers and streams. The species was once a very important bait minnow, and it was widely reared throughout the southeastern United States and sold to retail bait dealers. The popularity of the golden shiner has declined in the past 20 years, and only rarely is it available from minnow dealers. Recently, young common suckers, finescale dace, and fathead minnows have become the most popular bait species among anglers. Prof. Tom Waters of the University of Minnesota, an expert trout fisherman, has reported that golden shiners are great fighters on dry flies.

The golden shiner has a wide range from Saskatchewan to Quebec and southward to central Texas and Florida. It is common in some Minnesota lakes, such as Lake Minnetonka, but rare to occasional in many other lakes. The species seems to be more tolerant of low oxygen conditions and to nutrient enrichment than are most other native minnows.

Bullhead Minnow, *Pimephales vigilax* (Baird and Girard)

Scientific name: *Pimephales* = fat head (Greek); *vigilax* = watchful (Latin).

The bullhead minnow very closely resembles the bluntnose minnow and reaches a length of 3 inches. Its round snout, terminal mouth, short, S-shaped intestine, and silver **peritoneum** are characteristics that are useful in identifying the bullhead minnow and distinguishing it from the bluntnose minnow.

The bullhead minnow ranges from southern Minnesota to West Virginia and south to Alabama and to the Rio Grande drainage in Mexico. In Minnesota, it is found in the Mississippi River drainage south of Red Wing. There is also a single record from the Blue Earth River near Mankato.

The trivial name *vigilax* is the Latin for watchful or alert and refers to the behavior of the breeding male in guarding the nest and eggs.

Bluntnose minnow

Bluntnose Minnow, *Pimephales notatus* (Rafinesque)

Scientific name: *Pimephales* = fat head (Greek); *notatus* = marked (Latin).

The bluntnose minnow reaches a maximum length of 3 inches. Its body is elongate, and it has a blunt snout. The snout extends beyond the upper jaw and slightly overhangs the mouth. Its body is olive brown, with a prominent, dark lateral band that terminates in an equally prominent black spot at the base of the tail fin. The first ray of the dorsal fin, a rudimentary ray, is shorter and thicker than the first well-developed ray; these two rays are distinctly separated by a membrane. A prominent spot or blotch of pigment is present just above the anterior base of the dorsal fin.

The breeding male bluntnose minnow develops tubercles on the tip of its snout, and its head becomes swollen. He builds a nest under some object — a stick, a rock, a discarded can, a bit of broken crockery. In fact, almost any object can serve as a nest site. The female lays adhesive eggs that are fertilized by the male. He guards and tends the eggs until they hatch. Bluntnose minnows are herbivorous, feeding primarily on unicellular and filamentous algae, but they will eat all kinds of small animals.

The bluntnose minnow is widely distributed from North Dakota and Manitoba through the Great Lakes southward to Oklahoma and northern Alabama. It is common in small rivers and streams in Minnesota. It occurs frequently in northern lakes but is rare in large rivers.

Fathead minnow

Fathead Minnow, *Pimephales promelas* Rafinesque

Scientific name: *Pimephales* = fat head (Greek); *promelas* = before black (Greek), possibly referring to the darkened head of the original specimen.

The fathead minnow is one of the most common species of minnow in Minnesota waters. It is one of the hardiest of all bait minnows, and this quality has made it one of the best-known and most-used bait species.

The fathead minnow reaches a length of about 3 inches. The first ray of the dorsal fin is short and separated from the second ray by a distinct membrane. The dorsal fin has a black horizontal band across the middle. The anal fin has seven rays. The lateral line is incomplete, and the scales on the body are crowded anteriorly.

The fathead minnow displays sexual dimorphism, and, as in most fishes, this dimorphism is most pronounced at the time of spawning. The breeding male develops a tuberculate, spongy pad on its back between its head and the origin of the dorsal fin and two rows of tubercles across its snout between the upper lip and the nostrils. The sides of its body become blackish except for two wide, light-colored vertical bands. The female retains her drab coloration and changes only slightly in coloration with the changing seasons.

The male fathead minnow prepares a nesting site in the late spring on the underside of a board, a stone, a rock, a stick, or even a discarded can. The female deposits her adhesive eggs on the undersurface of the object, and the male fertilizes them. The female then leaves, and the male remains to guard the nest and the eggs. He constantly strokes the eggs with the spongy pad on his back. Every available nesting site may be occupied by the aggressive males; in fact, a rock or a board, when it is large enough, can be shared by several males. The males swim in and out of the nests and occasionally dash out to drive away other intruding males or potential egg predators. Spawning activity is most intense in the spring and early summer but continues until the autumn.

The fathead minnow is primarily a lake-and-stream fish. It survives well in ponds, ditches, and shallow lakes. These minnows are able to survive under conditions of very low oxygen concentration in both the winter and the summer and are among the last species of fish to die during winter and summer fish kills. Their ability to survive such stress may explain why there are small lakes that contain fathead minnows but no other fishes. Fathead minnows are easily reared and survive well in an aquarium with little care. The fathead minnow is primarily herbivorous but also eats aquatic worms, insects, and other animals. It has been used in the Twin Cities area to control mosquito populations in small lakes and ponds where other species of fishes do not survive.

The fathead minnow is common throughout the United States east of the Rocky Mountains, south into Mexico, and from northwestern Canada to Quebec. It has been widely introduced outside of its natural range.

Ozark Minnow, *Dionda nubila* (Forbes)

Scientific name: *Dionda* = from *Dione* (Greek), mother of Venus; *nubila* = dusky (Latin).

The Ozark minnow is 3 inches long and resembles superficially one of the shiners, or *Notropis*. It has a pronounced lateral band that extends anteriorly around the snout and encroaches on the chin and extends posteriorly and terminates in a dark tail spot. The body is silvery black above and silver to bronze below. The mouth is U shaped and terminal.

Ozark minnow

The Ozark minnow ranges from Wyoming to Illinois and south to the Ozarks. In Minnesota, it is common to the headwaters of the Zumbro River in Dodge and Olmsted counties and in the Cedar River in Mower County.

Shiners, Genus *Notropis* Rafinesque

The genus *Notropis* includes more than 100 species of small minnows, commonly referred to as shiners, which are found throughout eastern North America. Eighteen species of shiners are found in Minnesota waters, the largest number of species in any of the genera of fishes known from Minnesota, in fact, more species than in most fish families native to the state. The genus was first described by the famous Constantine Rafinesque in his classic *Ichthyologia Ohioensis*, published in 1820. The name *Notropis* translates from the Greek as back keel. The name, unfortunately, was based on a dried and shriveled specimen that Rafinesque used as the type for the generic name. Shiners in general lack a keel on the back. This was not the first nor the last time that a generic name was based on an aberrant specimen. In Rafinesque's time, the early decades of the nineteenth century, naturalists either preserved small specimens in spirits or dried them. Even specimens in spirits became dehydrated after months out in the wilderness of the Ohio River valley. Large specimens were dried; and, in many cases, only the skin, the head, and a few bones were saved for the museum collection. The naturalists made careful notes on colors of the specimens, measurements of body proportions, palatability, and uses made of the fishes by native Americans. The specimen or specimens and the notes were the foundations for descriptions of the species new to science that were published in scientific journals of the time. Often, the naturalists provided only rather brief and cryptic notes and a less-than-revealing sketch of the fish. In many instances, the collector was not the describer, but a professional hired by a prominent scientist to collect various plants and animals for the scientist or for the institution with which the scientist was associated. What is most significant, however, is the scientific acuity of the early naturalists, some of whom were self-trained. The fact that they erred so seldom is truly remarkable, especially when one considers the hardships and primitive conditions naturalists, such as Rafinesque, experienced in their search for the new and fascinating creatures of the New World.

Pallid Shiner, *Notropis amnis* Hubbs and Greene

Scientific name: *Notropis* = back keel (Greek); *amnis* = of the river (Latin).

The pallid shiner is a small fish that reaches a maximum length of about 2½ inches. Its body is silvery, with a thin lateral band that extends onto the head. Its snout is blunt and overhangs the mouth.

The pallid shiner ranges from southern Minnesota to Indiana and southward to eastern Texas. It is rare in Minnesota, restricted to the Mississippi River and the mouths of the larger tributary streams south of the Twin Cities. Wisconsin fishery biologists have collected the pallid shiner from the St. Croix River. The rarity may only be apparent; the large river habitat is difficult to sample adequately for small fishes such as the pallid shiner.

Pugnose Shiner, *Notropis anogenus* Forbes

Scientific name: *Notropis* = back keel (Greek); *anogenus* = without a chin (Greek).

The pugnose shiner is a small, moderately stout shiner that reaches a length of 2 inches. Its body coloration is dusky silver, and there is a dark lateral band that extends down the side of the body from the tip of the snout through the eye to the base of the tail fin. The chin is pigmented, and the peritoneum, the lining of the body cavity, is black. The most striking feature of this shiner is its very small, terminal mouth that curves upward at a sharp angle, giving the fish a pug-nosed appearance.

The pugnose shiner is one of Minnesota's rarest shiners. It is widely distributed in weedy lakes and streams, but it is never abundant. One rarely takes more than two or three individuals in a collection, even with intensive sampling. The elimination of rooted aquatic plants to create swimming beaches has probably contributed to the decline in abundance of this interesting little minnow. Today, the species is more common in Minnesota waters than in the waters of other states where it was once very common. Recent regulations and laws that have reduced indiscriminate habitat modification may ensure the survival of the pugnose shiner in Minnesota waters.

The pugnose shiner originally ranged from North Dakota eastward through Illinois, Indiana, and Ohio to the St. Lawrence drainage; today, it occurs only in parts of Michigan, Wisconsin, and Minnesota. We have no specimens from the Lake Superior drainage, but the species is, or at least was, present in all the other drainage systems in Minnesota.

Emerald Shiner, *Notropis atherinoides* Rafinesque

Scientific name: *Notropis* = back keel (Greek); *atherinoides* = silversidelike (Greek).

The emerald shiner is a slender species that reaches a length of about 4 inches. The body is translucent green above and silvery below. The eyes are large, their diameter about equal to the length of the snout.

Emerald shiner

The emerald shiner is an inhabitant of lakes and large rivers, but it sometimes enters the mouths of smaller streams in late autumn and winter. When these shiners are present in large schools, they shimmer and sparkle as the sun strikes their emerald dorsal surfaces and their silvery sides. Superficially, they resemble members of the silverside family, Atherinidae; hence comes the trivial name *atherinoides*, silversidelike.

Emerald shiners feed largely on plankton and occasionally on insects on the water surface. They are spring spawners. These attractive fish are important forage, but they are not hardy and die quickly in the confines of a minnow bucket or a box.

The emerald shiner ranges from northwestern Canada to Lake Champlain and southward to Texas and Virginia. It is present in all the drainage systems in Minnesota.

River Shiner, *Notropis blennius* (Girard)

Scientific name: *Notropis* = back keel (Greek); *blennius* = a fish (Latin).

The river shiner is a small shiner, 2½ inches in length, with a pale olive back and silver sides. A silvery lateral band is present on both sides. As its common name implies, the river shiner is most frequently found in rivers. It is found only rarely in lakes.

The river shiner ranges from Alberta and Wyoming east to Pennsylvania and south to Texas and Tennessee. It is common in the Mississippi River from Lake Pepin southward and in the Rainy River. It is less common in the Minnesota River and in the St. Croix River south of Taylors Falls.

The trivial name *blennius*, coined by Girard, refers to the similarity between the river shiner and a marine fish known as the blenny.

Mimic Shiner, *Notropis volucellus* (Cope)

Scientific name: *Notropis* = back keel (Greek); *volucellus* = swift (Latin).

The mimic shiner is a small, silvery *Notropis* that reaches a length of about 2½ inches. Its back is dusky, and its faint, rather diffuse lateral band is restricted to the body and does not en-

Mimic shiner

croach on the head. The mimic shiner resembles the sand and bigmouth shiners.

Mimic shiners are usually pelagic, living in open water, during the day and move in to the shore region at night. A detailed study of the mimic shiner carried out by Prof. Peter Moyle of the University of California at Davis on Long Lake, Clearwater County, revealed that this shiner feeds on insect pupae, mayfly adults, and certain crustaceans.

Large schools of mimic shiners can be seen in the open water of a lake, sometimes miles from shore. Occasionally, the angler may see the school disperse — suddenly, the fish are dashing off in all directions, some breaking through the surface and into the air. Sometimes, the observer may even see the large predator, a perch or a walleye, that triggered the escape response. Shortly after it dispersed, the school reforms, only to be dispersed again. Fishes, including the mimic shiner, produce chemical substances when frightened that are detected by their associates in the school; and, depending on the stimulus, the individuals disperse or form a very tight school. If an individual from the school should be wounded by a predator, the stimulus to flee is particularly strong. It seems that there *is* safety in numbers. When one has the opportunity to see such a dispersal of individuals in the school, the reason for the trivial name *volucellus*, meaning winged or swift, becomes apparent.

The mimic shiner ranges from Lake of the Woods through

Bigmouth shiner

Canada to the upper St. Lawrence drainage and south through Minnesota to Alabama and central Texas. It is present in all of Minnesota but the Missouri River drainage system in the extreme southwestern corner of the state. The mimic shiner inhabits lakes and large rivers.

Bigmouth Shiner, *Notropis dorsalis* (Agassiz)

Scientific name: *Notropis* = back keel (Greek); *dorsalis* = of the back (Latin).

The bigmouth shiner is medium-size shiner that reaches a length of 3 inches. It has silvery sides and a dusky back. The scales posterior to the head are crowded, and occasionally the region of the nape may be scaleless. The head is quite large, and the snout overhangs the mouth slightly. In profile, the ventral surface of the head is flattened. Bigmouth shiners are easily confused with sand and mimic shiners, and even the skilled ichthyologist may have to look twice to be certain which species he or she has in hand.

The bigmouth shiner is distributed from Wyoming and Colorado through Minnesota and Missouri and the southern Great Lakes region to New York and Pennsylvania. In Minnesota, it is most common in sand-bottomed streams tributary to the Red, Minnesota, St. Croix, Mississippi, and Missouri rivers. It is not known from the Lake Superior drainage in Minnesota.

Sand shiner

Sand Shiner, *Notropis stramineus* (Cope)

Scientific name: *Notropis* = back keel (Greek);
stramineus = of straw (Latin), referring to the color of
preserved specimens.

The sand shiner is a medium-size minnow that reaches a
length of about 2½ inches. It has a vague lateral band and a
dorsal stripe down the middle of its back anterior to the dorsal
fin. The body is silvery, with a pale greenish back when alive;
after preservation, it takes on a straw color. The sand shiner
resembles the bigmouth and mimic shiners, and occasionally all
three may be taken in the same collection. There are a number of
books on fishes, including *Northern Fishes* (Eddy and Underhill,
1974), in which one can find a key for identifying the three
species and in which the distinguishing characteristics are discussed and listed.

The sand shiner is distributed from North Dakota to the St.
Lawrence and Ohio River drainages and south to Mexico. The
sand shiner is common throughout Minnesota with the exception of the Lake Superior drainage, but the species is found in
the latter drainage in Wisconsin and upper-peninsula Michigan.
Its preferred habitat is streams and rivers, and only rarely does it
occur in lakes, except in river lakes such as Lake St. Croix and
Lake Pepin.

Common Shiner, *Notropis cornutus* (Mitchill)

Scientific name: *Notropis* = back keel;
cornutus = horned (Latin).

The common shiner, one of the larger species of shiner, may reach a length of 12 inches, but it is usually 3 to 5 inches long. Its body is silvery, with a greenish back. The scales of the common shiner are distinctly elongated vertically, and in the adult the scales along the lateral line have a shaggy appearance.

The common shiner spawns in late May and early June. The males develop rosy pigmentation on their bellies and paired fins, and they acquire large tubercles on their heads. The males construct nests of small piles of pebbles and gravel at the tops of shallow riffles. At the nests, they court females and defend the sites against the incursions of other males. When spawning is at its peak, there is tremendous activity in the riffle, with courting behavior, nest building, and territory defending going on. Once spawning has been completed, the males desert the riffle nest sites and disperse throughout the stream. The nesting materials may then be appropriated by other species of minnows such as the blacknose dace and the rosyface shiner.

The common shiner is an important forage fish for larger predaceous fishes, but it does not survive well in confinement. Hence, it is of little value as a bait fish. Large common shiners

Common shiner

occasionally will take a small spinner, fly, or baited hook. Like one of the authors, children who have caught these shiners and cooked them over an open fire can attest to their tastiness. To the adult who has eaten the more toothsome trout, the common shiner is only a nuisance.

The common shiner is distributed from Saskatchewan to Quebec, south to Colorado, Kansas, and the Gulf Coast drainage. It is widely distributed throughout Minnesota in lakes and streams, but it is more common in streams.

Weed Shiner, *Notropis texanus* (Girard)

Scientific name: *Notropis* = back keel (Greek); *texanus* = named for Texas, where Girard collected specimens.

The weed shiner is a small, black-banded minnow that reaches a maximum length of 2½ inches. It can be easily confused with the blackchin shiner, but the weed shiner usually has seven anal rays and the blackchin shiner has eight. The lateral band on the weed shiner is more diffuse and does not display the prominent zigzag appearance of the band on the blackchin shiner.

The weed shiner ranges from the Red River in Minnesota east to Michigan and south to Florida and Texas. The only locality in Minnesota where large numbers of weed shiners are found is the Otter Tail River, a tributary of the Red River in west-central Minnesota. As its common name implies, the weed shiner can be found in weedy areas of the river.

Topeka Shiner, *Notropis topeka* Gilbert

Scientific name: *Notropis* = back keel (Greek); *topeka* = named for Topeka, Kansas, where the specimens used to name the species were collected.

This attractive little shiner is restricted to southwestern Minnesota in Rock Creek and its tributaries, which drain into the Missouri River through the Big Sioux River. The Topeka shiner rarely reaches a length of 2 inches. Its deep body is dusky silver in color, and its snout is blunt. A prominent lateral band terminates in a small, black tail spot.

Of all the fishes discussed so far, no other species has a similar distribution pattern. The Topeka shiner is a prairie species, restricted in its distribution to Iowa, South Dakota, Nebraska, Kansas, Missouri, and southwestern Minnesota. There is evidence that it is less abundant in prairie streams than it once was, perhaps as a result of agricultural development and climatic change.

Rosyface Shiner, *Notropis rubellus* (Agassiz)

Scientific name: *Notropis* = back keel (Greek);
rubellus = reddish (Latin).

The rosyface shiner reaches a maximum length of 3 inches. It has an elliptical body that is olive colored above and silvery below, with an evident lateral band. The snout is pointed and longer than the diameter of the eye. The rosyface shiner resembles the emerald shiner but has a longer and sharper snout, and

Rosyface shiner

Rosyface shiner showing red breeding color

the body of the emerald shiner is deeper than that of the rosyface shiner. In late May and June, breeding males have blood red ventral fins and a dark red stripe that extends from the operculum, or gill cover, along the side of the belly to the pelvic fins. Females lack the intense red color but may have a slight rosy pink tinge.

The rosyface shiner ranges from North Dakota and Manitoba to the St. Lawrence and Hudson rivers, southward to Virginia and throughout the Ohio River drainage. In Minnesota, it is found in the tributaries of the Mississippi River south of St. Anthony Falls, in the Minnesota River, and in the Red River.

Spotfin Shiner, *Notropis spilopterus* (Cope)

Scientific name: *Notropis* = back keel (Greek); *spilopterus* = spotfin (Greek).

The spotfin shiner is a small minnow, usually less than 4 inches long, that is common in the large rivers and streams of Minnesota with the exception of the Lake Superior and Rainy River drainage systems. As its common name suggests, it has a black blotch of pigment on the membranes between the last three rays of the dorsal fin. In very small individuals, the spot may be faint or obscure. This minnow is deep bodied, with a

Spotfin shiner

silvery sheen, and it has a black vertical bar posterior to the operculum. In live specimens, the scales have a diamond shape and each scale is outlined with black pigment. In late spring and early summer, the breeding males become heavily pigmented and steel bluish in color; their ventral fins become dull yellow to bright yellow. The head and fins are profusely covered with small tubercles, and the fish feels rough, like sandpaper.

The spotfin shiner is an important forage fish for larger fishes, but it is of little value as a bait minnow. It does not live long under the crowded conditions that exist in minnow holding tanks. They survive well in small aquariums and feed on brine shrimp and dried fish food.

The range of the spotfin shiner extends from the Red River drainage in North Dakota and Minnesota, east through southern Ontario to the Potomac River, and south to eastern Oklahoma, northern Arkansas, and northern Alabama.

Red Shiner, *Notropis lutrensis* (Baird and Girard)

Scientific name: *Notropis* = back keel (Greek);
lutrensis = from *lutra,* meaning otter (Latin), referring to
Otter Creek in Arkansas, where the species
was first collected.

The red shiner is a small, deep-bodied shiner that reaches a length of about 3 inches. Its body is steel blue above and silvery below; its fins have a distinct reddish tinge. The red shiner's appearance is similar to the spotfin shiner's, but the red shiner has a blunter snout and lacks a pigment spot on the posterior portion of the dorsal fin. A breeding male red shiner has bright orange red ventral fins and a dark vertical bar on its side just posterior to the operculum. Small tubercles are present on the male's body, giving it the texture of fine sandpaper.

The red shiner ranges from Wyoming to southwestern Minnesota, through Iowa and Illinois, and southward to Mexico. In Minnesota, the red shiner is found only in the Missouri River drainage in the extreme southwestern counties of Pipestone, Rock, and Nobles.

Redfin Shiner, *Notropis umbratilis* (Girard)

Scientific name: *Notropis* = back keel (Greek);
umbratilis = from *umbra,* meaning a shade (Latin).

The redfin shiner is another deep-bodied shiner with a blunt snout. It reaches a maximum length of about 3½ inches. Its body is steel blue, with a silvery belly. An identifying characteristic is a dark splotch at the anterior base of the dorsal fin. Breeding male redfin shiners are colored a spectacular iridescent blue, their bodies are covered with fine tubercles, and their fins are dusky red. Females are more subdued in color but may have a few tubercles.

The redfin shiner ranges from southeastern Minnesota and eastern Kansas through the Great Lakes drainage, southward to Texas, Kentucky, and West Virginia. In Minnesota, it is restricted to the Zumbro, Root, and Cedar rivers and their tributaries in the southeastern part of the state.

Spottail Shiner, *Notropis hudsonius* (Clinton)

Scientific name: *Notropis* = back keel (Greek);
hudsonius = named for the Hudson River, where the species was first collected.

The spottail shiner is a medium-size minnow that reaches a length of about 4 inches. It is a silvery minnow that has a prominent black spot at the base of the tail fin. The black tail spot is most distinctive. In contrast to other shiners with a tail spot, the spottail shiner lacks a lateral band and stripe. Its back is a light greenish color and is often iridescent. Young spottail shiners may have a slight dusting of black pigment.

The spottail shiner is widely distributed in North America, from the Northwest Territories in Canada to North Dakota, east to the Hudson River and southeast through Iowa to Georgia. In Minnesota, it is common in all drainage basins, especially in Lake of the Woods, Lake St. Croix, and Lake Pepin. It appears to be intolerant of silt-laden and polluted waters.

Governor DeWitt Clinton of New York, an early contributor to

Spottail shiner

ichthyology, an accomplished naturalist, and a scientist, first described the spottail shiner as *Clupea hudsonius* in 1824 in the *Annals Lyceum of Natural History of New York*. Having been named by DeWitt Clinton, the spottail shiner has the distinction of being the only Minnesota fish named by a person who was a candidate for the office of president of the United States.

Blacknose Shiner, *Notropis heterolepis* Eigenmann and Eigenmann

Scientific name: *Notropis* = back keel (Greek); *heterolepis* = varying scale (Greek).

The blacknose shiner is a small fish that reaches a maximum length of 2½ inches. It is characterized by a lateral band that extends from the tail fin through the eye and over the snout but not as far as the chin. The pigment forming the lateral band is composed of a row of crescent-shaped marks formed by the

Blacknose shiner

dark edges of the scales in the lateral line. The unpigmented chin and the crescent marks serve to distinguish the blacknose shiner from the blackchin shiner.

The blacknose shiner ranges from Saskatchewan to Nova Scotia, south to Iowa and east through the Iowa River drainage. Its preferred habitat is clean, weedy lakes and streams in the glacial lakes region of Minnesota. Weed removal, eutrophication, and other habitat modifications have resulted in the disappearance of this attractive little shiner from the southern lake region in Minnesota and from Iowa and Ohio.

Blackchin Shiner, *Notropis heterodon* (Cope)

Scientific name: *Notropis* = back keel (Greek); *heterodon* = varying tooth (Greek).

The blackchin shiner is a small fish that rarely reaches a length of 2½ inches. Its body is bronze to olive yellow above, with silvery sides and belly. A dusky lateral stripe extends from the tail fin forward through the eye and over the snout and encroaches on the chin. The latter characteristic, the black chin, gives the species its common name and is clearly distinctive. Another telling feature is the zigzag appearance of the lateral band, which is produced by the dark edges of the scales in the lateral line alternating with the dark edges of the scale row above.

The blackchin shiner is distributed from North Dakota to Quebec and south to Iowa and New York. It is characteristic of the glacial lake districts of eastern North America. The blackchin has been found to be most abundant in the lake region of the northern half of Minnesota, usually in lakes but occasionally in streams connected to lakes, such as the Crow Wing and Otter Tail rivers.

Pugnose Minnow, *Notropis emiliae* (Hay)

Scientific name: *Notropis* = back keel (Greek); *emiliae* = named for Mrs. Emily Hay.

The pugnose minnow reaches a maximum length of 4 inches. Its body is yellowish to silver, and a dusky lateral band terminates in a dark spot at the base of the tail fin. As its common name implies, the fish's snout is blunt, but more obvious is its small upturned mouth, which is almost vertical. The dorsal fin has nine rays. Breeding males have dusky pigmented areas on the anterior and posterior membranes of their dorsal fins, with clear, windowlike areas in the middle of the fins.

The pugnose minnow is distributed from southern Minnesota, east to Michigan and south to Texas and Florida. It is present in the sloughs and backwaters of the Mississippi River of southern Minnesota. Specimens have been collected from the Root and Zumbro rivers in southeastern Minnesota. Recently, fishery biologists from the Ecological Services Section of the Minnesota DNR have collected specimens in the Mississippi River north of Red Wing. These specimens represent the most northern record of the species.

Brassy Minnow, *Hybognathus hankinsoni* Hubbs

Scientific name: *Hybognathus* = bulging jaw (Greek); *hankinsoni* = named for T. L. Hankinson, an American scientist.

The brassy minnow is one of Minnesota's most common and widely distributed minnows. Its range is from Montana to Lake Champlain and southward to Nebraska, Missouri, and Colorado. It reaches a total length of 3 to 4 inches. As its common name

Brassy minnow

implies, when it is alive, the body is yellowish and quite brassy in appearance. Members of the genus have blunt snouts. The brassy minnow is named in honor of T. L. Hankinson, a professor of zoology at the University of North Dakota who carried out an early survey of the fishes of that state.

Silver Minnow, *Hybognathus nuchalis* Agassiz

Scientific name: *Hybognathus* = bulging jaw (Greek); *nuchalis* = of the nape (Latin).

This silvery minnow reaches a length of about 5 inches. It resembles in many ways the brassy minnow, but, as its common name implies, it is silvery in color, rather than yellowish. It also has a longer and more pointed snout than the brassy minnow does. Silver minnows are characteristic inhabitants of large rivers and the mouths of tributaries to the Minnesota River and Mississippi River south of St. Anthony Falls. It is also found in the floodplain lakes south of Hastings, Minnesota.

The fish's geographic range includes the Missouri River drainage of Montana and to the east the Connecticut River system and to the south the Gulf of Mexico drainage.

Common Stoneroller, *Campostoma anomalum*
(Rafinesque)

Scientific name: *Campostoma* = curved mouth (Greek); *anomalum* = unusual, abnormal (Greek).

The common stoneroller is another large minnow. It reaches a length of 8 to 10 inches. The body is brownish black and more or less mottled. The genus to which it belongs is characterized by a cartilaginous ridge in the lower jaw. Another unusual anatomical anomaly of the fish is its intestine, which is wrapped around its swim bladder several times.

Stonerollers spawn in June and early July. The males develop large tubercles on their heads, their backs, and their sides as well as on their dorsal fins. Both the dorsal and anal fins of the male develop reddish brown or orangish bands on each side of a dark crossbar. The females lack the tubercles but do develop some pigmentation on their fins. The stonerollers are nest build-

Common stoneroller

Largescale stoneroller

ers, and the males carry small pebbles to a gravelly area, eventually constructing a pile of pebbles almost 2 feet in diameter. The females deposit their eggs in the piles of stones, the males fertilize them, and the eggs settle into the protective crevices.

The common stoneroller ranges from Minnesota over the Great Plains to Texas and eastward to the Atlantic Coast. It prefers creeks and small rivers to lakes and very large rivers. It is present in all but the Lake Superior drainage in Minnesota, and it is more common in the Minnesota River and the Mississippi River south of St. Anthony Falls than elsewhere.

Largescale Stoneroller, *Campostoma oligolepis* Hubbs and Greene

Scientific name: *Campostoma* = curved mouth (Greek); *oligolepis* = few scales (Greek).

The largescale stoneroller is similar to the common stoneroller and until a few years ago was treated as a subspecies of *C. anomalum.* The differences between the two species are technical ones not obvious to the casual viewer. The largescale stoneroller has larger and so fewer scales in the lateral line series than the common stoneroller. *C. oligolepis* has 43 to 47 scales in the lateral line and 31 to 36 circumference scales; *C. anomalum* has 47 to 55 lateral-line scales and 39 to 46 circumference scales. Using these characteristics, even ichthyologists have experienced difficulty in recognizing the largescale stoneroller. But, when the sum of the two counts is used, the difficulty is reduced. The ranges of the sums of lateral-line and circumference scales are 74 to 82 for *C. oligolepis* and 87 to 102 for *C. anomalum*.

The largescale stoneroller is represented by two populations: one in Minnesota, Wisconsin, northern Iowa, and northern Illinois and one in Missouri and northern Arkansas. In Minnesota, the largescale stoneroller is restricted to the Root River and the south branch of the Zumbro River. It occurs in company with the common stoneroller, but there is no interbreeding.

Family CATOSTOMIDAE
The Suckers

The family Catostomidae contains approximately 60 kinds of freshwater fishes commonly called suckers. Suckers are found in both Asia and North America. Although they are much more diverse today in North America than in Asia, it is thought that they originated in Asia and that the ancestors of today's North American species migrated across the Bering Straits.

Suckers are closely related to minnows, and they resemble them physically. Suckers have soft-rayed fins and toothless jaws, and most, though not all, of them have thick-lipped (suckerlike) mouths. Their numerous pharyngeal teeth are comblike or knoblike and are arranged in a single series; by contrast, the pharyngeal teeth of minnows, which are fewer in number, are arranged in one, two, or three rows. Suckers have more than 10 dorsal fin rays, whereas native North American minnows have 10 or fewer. The introduced carp and goldfish are minnows that have more than 10 dorsal fin rays, but these two fishes also have stout hard rays at the front of the dorsal and anal fins. All suckers lack hard rays.

Sixteen kinds of suckers are definitely known to occur in Minnesota, and another, the black buffalo, probably occurs in the southern portion of the state in the Mississippi River system. Some suckers are most common in large rivers in Minnesota, and others live in lakes and streams. The white sucker is among the most widely distributed and abundant fishes in the state, and the bigmouth buffalo and some kinds of redhorses are also common in many places. Others, such as the blue sucker, apparently reach the northern limits of their range in Minnesota and are also sensitive to pollution, with the result that they are rare in the state.

Because of their abundance, the common kinds of suckers play an important role in the freshwater environment. They feed mostly by sucking in nutrient-rich ooze and small plants and animals from the bottom or by straining tiny plants and animals from the water. In turn, they themselves become food for predaceous fishes, such as walleyes, northern pike, and several kinds of basses. Suckers such as buffalofishes and carpsuckers are commonly netted or trapped by commercial fishermen. They are used as food for people or are processed into animal feed. Suckers are good to eat when baked, smoked, fried, or pickled.

Bigmouth Buffalo, *Ictiobus cyprinellus* (Valenciennes)

Scientific name: *Ictiobus* = bull fish (Greek); *cyprinellus* = small carp (Latin).

The most common and widely distributed buffalofish in Minnesota, the bigmouth buffalo occurs in the state from the Red River drainage southward and eastward through the Minnesota and Mississippi River systems. It is not known from the Lake Superior drainage. Its overall range is from Saskatchewan to Lake Erie and south to the Gulf of Mexico. The typical habitats of the bigmouth buffalo are large rivers, lakes, and sloughs. It is most common in Minnesota today in the St. Croix and lower Mississippi rivers, where it is harvested commercially in a

Bigmouth buffalo

quantity second only to that of the carp. In this century, droughts and the digging of drainage ditches have eliminated shallow lakes in central and southern Minnesota that formerly provided good habitats for this species.

The largest sucker in Minnesota, where it occasionally reaches 50 pounds, the bigmouth buffalo is a heavy-bodied fish with a long dorsal fin (having more than 20 rays) and large scales. It is greenish to blackish on the back and sides, with a coppery sheen, and lighter below. Its most distinctive characteristic is its thin-lipped, terminal mouth, which contrasts with the **subterminal** mouth of the other Minnesota suckers, including the closely related smallmouth buffalo.

With its terminal mouth and long gill rakers, the bigmouth buffalo is well equipped to filter small, suspended animals from the water as it swims along and to forage off the bottom as well. It eats vegetation and various small aquatic animals, such as insect larvae, mollusks, and crustaceans. It is often found in schools. It seldom bites on a hook but is sometimes caught with dough balls. It is the most commonly eaten sucker in Minnesota and is usually prepared by being stuffed and baked.

The bigmouth buffalo spawns in April and May in Minnesota. As a prelude to spawning, adults migrate into shallow bays or through small tributary streams to sloughs. The females deposit their eggs over vegetation, rocks, and mud, and the eggs receive no parental care. The young hatch in about 10 days. The spawning run of buffalofishes can be a spectacular sight as great numbers of fishes, many with their backs out of the water, crowd their way through tiny outlets leading to sloughs. These runs are less frequent today than in the past, but substantial numbers of buffalofishes are still trapped while making their spawning runs.

Smallmouth Buffalo, *Ictiobus bubalus* (Rafinesque)

Scientific name: *Ictiobus* = bull fish (Greek); *bubalus* = buffalo (Greek).

The smallmouth buffalo inhabits lakes and large rivers in southern Minnesota. It is most common in the St. Croix and lower Mississippi rivers, especially in the clear, slow-moving waters of Lake St. Croix and Lake Pepin. It has been reported from the Minnesota River, but it has not been found there in recent years. It is far less abundant in Minnesota than the bigmouth buffalo. It ranges from Saskatchewan southward through the Midwest to Mexico.

The smallmouth buffalo is smaller than the bigmouth buffalo. Although it occasionally reaches 50 pounds south of Minnesota, it seldom exceeds 5 pounds in the state. It is similar in color to the bigmouth buffalo and is most easily distinguished from its larger relative by its small, thick-lipped, subterminal mouth. Commercial fishermen usually market the smallmouth buffalo along with the bigmouth buffalo. It is less important as a food fish in Minnesota than the bigmouth buffalo simply because it is less common.

A bottom feeder, the smallmouth buffalo eats insect larvae, snails, vegetation, and debris. It spawns in the early summer in Minnesota, where it sometimes joins the bigmouth buffalo and the carp in making spawning runs up streams that lead to the sloughs where spawning takes place.

Blue Sucker, *Cycleptus elongatus* (LeSueur)

Scientific name: *Cycleptus* = small round mouth (according to its author); *elongatus* = elongate.

The blue sucker is among the rarest of Minnesota's fishes. It is known in the state from the St. Croix and lower Mississippi rivers, in which specimens are occasionally reported by commercial fishermen and DNR personnel. It occurs over the south-central United States and extends its range northward in the Missouri and Mississippi river basins. It goes all the way to northern Montana in the Missouri system and apparently reaches the northern limits of its range in the Mississippi system in Minnesota. It is usually found in swift-flowing channels of large rivers and streams over rocky or gravelly bottoms. Although it lives in reservoirs created by dams on the Missouri River, it does not tolerate heavy pollution and siltation and is apparently becoming increasingly rare throughout most of its range. Because of its sensitivity, the blue sucker can serve as a guide to judging water quality — one can be sure that, when the blue sucker thrives, the environment is healthy.

An elongated, cylindrical fish that reaches a length of about 2 feet, the blue sucker is dark blue or olive above and whitish below. It can be distinguished from other Minnesota suckers by its having the combination of a long dorsal fin (with more than 20 rays) and small scales (more than 50 in the lateral line).

Little is known about the habits of the blue sucker. It feeds mostly on small organisms and debris that it takes from the bottom. It spawns in the early summer in shallow places in rivers.

Highfin Carpsucker, *Carpiodes velifer* (Rafinesque)

Scientific name: *Carpiodes* = carplike (Latin);
velifer = sail bearer (Latin).

The highfin carpsucker is known in Minnesota from the St. Croix, Minnesota, and lower Mississippi rivers and their tributaries and from lakes in the southern half of the state. Past accounts suggest that it was formerly locally abundant in the Mississippi and its tributaries in Minnesota, but it seems uncommon there today. As with other suckers, it appears that the declining quality of its habitat has significantly reduced its numbers. It reaches the northern limits of its range in Minnesota and ranges southward to the Gulf of Mexico.

Carpsuckers resemble buffalofishes in having long dorsal fins and deep bodies, but they are less robust than buffalofishes. Both the highfin carpsucker and the river carpsucker attain a length of about a foot in Minnesota and are brownish on the back, silvery on the sides, and whitish on the belly. The mouth in both species is small and subterminal; the lower lip often has

Highfin carpsucker

a small knob, or button, at its tip; and the lateral line has 33 to 37 scales along it. The highfin carpsucker is so named because the fin rays at the front of the dorsal fin are distinctly elongated (these fin rays are short in young individuals and grow disproportionately with age). The river carpsucker has short dorsal fin rays. Another close relative, the quillback, has a longer snout and 35 to 39 scales along the lateral line. The rays at the front of the dorsal fin vary in length in the quillback but are often long enough to resemble closely those of the highfin carpsucker. Carpsuckers are so hard to tell apart, especially when small, that even experts can have difficulty; in fact, much confusion about the distribution of carpsuckers and other suckers has resulted from misidentifications and the acceptance of identifications that could not be confirmed with actual specimens.

The highfin carpsucker is apparently a bottom feeder, but it sometimes swims along just below the surface of the water, with its dorsal fin exposed. Adults in spawning condition have been taken over gravelly riffles of rivers.

River Carpsucker, *Carpiodes carpio* (Rafinesque)

Scientific name: *Carpiodes* = carplike (Latin); *carpio* = carp (Latin).

The river carpsucker lives in large rivers in southern Minnesota. Its range is from Montana through the Midwest and south to Mexico. It closely resembles the highfin carpsucker but has

River carpsucker

shorter fin rays at the front of the dorsal fin. It lives in schools, usually in sluggish water, and feeds from the bottom. It spawns in the spring and early summer.

Quillback, *Carpiodes cyprinus* (LeSueur)

Scientific name: *Carpiodes* = carplike (Latin); *cyprinus* = named after the generic name of the carp.

The quillback lives in lakes and streams over most of Minnesota except the Lake Superior drainage. It seems most common in rivers in the southern half of the state. Past reports suggest that it was once common in Lake of the Woods, and it still forms part of the commercial catch in the Red Lakes. Its range is across much of southern Canada eastward to the east coast of the United States and southward to the Gulf of Mexico in Alabama.

The quillback attains a length of about 2 feet in Minnesota. It is usually silvery, but specimens from many places, such as Lake St. Croix, are distinctly yellow. The quillback seems far more common in Minnesota today than the highfin and river carpsuckers. It has a slightly longer snout and more lateral line scales (35 to 39) than these other two and usually lacks a knob on the lower lip. The length of the rays at the front of the dorsal fin is variable, and some individuals have long dorsal fin rays just as the highfin carpsucker does.

Except when spawning, when it enters deep, gravelly riffles, the quillback is usually found in quiet water. In breeding season, adult carpsuckers, especially the males, temporarily develop small tubercles on their heads, scales, and fins. The quillback has bigger tubercles than the highfin and river carpsuckers.

Spotted Sucker, *Minytrema melanops* (Rafinesque)

Scientific name: *Minytrema* = reduced aperture (Greek), referring to the reduced lateral line; *melanops* = black appearance (Greek).

The spotted sucker is found in the St. Croix and lower Mississippi rivers in Minnesota. It was collected in the Minnesota River in the 1890s but has not been noted there recently. It ranges from southern Minnesota eastward to Pennsylvania and southward to the southeastern seaboard and the Gulf of Mexico. Its decline has been noted in the eastern sector of its range, and it has probably been affected by the pollution and siltation of rivers. It usually lives in slow-moving water in large rivers, sloughs, and river lakes such as Lake St. Croix and Lake Pepin, but it spawns over riffles. The northernmost record of this species in Minnesota is based on the observation by DNR personnel of adults spawning over riffles just below the dam on the St. Croix at Taylors Falls in Chisago County in early May 1968.

Quillback

The spotted sucker attains a length of about 20 inches in Minnesota. It is brownish above and white below, with silvery or brassy sides. The scales on the back and sides each bear a dark spot at their base, forming a series of stripelike rows of spots along the body. These rows of spots help distinguish the spotted sucker from other suckers, although they are sometimes obscured by surrounding pigmentation in adults and are weakly developed in young individuals. In adults, the lateral line is reduced and is found on only a few scales along the side. The mouth is subterminal and the lips are thin. The spotted sucker eats bottom debris and various small animals, such as insect larvae.

On spawning riffles, males court females by prodding them and swimming back and forth over them. Spawning is most often accomplished through the teamwork of trios of two males and one female. The males position themselves on either side of the female and press against her, and the three fish vibrate their bodies to stimulate the release of eggs and milt. The vibrations stir sediment that helps conceal the eggs when it settles. The eggs drift and settle among rocks and gravel, where they are left unattended until they hatch.

Northern Hog Sucker, *Hypentelium nigricans* (LeSueur)

Scientific name: *Hypentelium* = below five lobes (Greek), referring to the lobes on the lower lip; *nigricans* = blackish (Latin).

The northern hog sucker is rather common in Minnesota in small, clear tributary streams of the Minnesota, St. Croix, and lower Mississippi rivers. Its presence in the Red River system in Minnesota and in the Mississippi above St. Anthony Falls in Minneapolis has only recently been verified. It is not known from the Rainy River and Lake Superior drainages. Its range is from Minnesota eastward into New York and southward as far as Oklahoma and Georgia.

A strange-looking fish with a large head that is concave between the eyes, large pectoral fins, and a tapering body, the

Northern hog sucker

northern hog sucker is generally found in shallow riffles over gravel and rubble from spring through autumn in Minnesota. It is known to enter quiet pools for refuge in the winter. It is brownish or greenish above and white below and is mottled with four to six darkly pigmented bars (called saddles) that extend across the back and down the sides. With its specialized body shape and camouflaging coloration, it is well suited for life in the riffle habitat, where it can usually be found resting on the bottom. It moves about by darting quickly from one place to another. When it comes to rest, it is easily lost from sight again, even though it may be as much as 20 inches long.

The mouth of the northern hog sucker is subterminal, with thick lips. The fish feeds by overturning stones and by disturbing bottom sediments to obtain small organisms, such as insect larvae.

The northern hog sucker spawns in the late spring in Minnesota. Solitary for most of the year, northern hog suckers congregate in shallow riffles to spawn and exhibit lively behavior as they splash and chase about. Females are larger than males, and each spawning female is attended by at least one male and often by two. The spawning fish vibrate their bodies and in the process form the shallow depressions in which the eggs are deposited. Males attending females are often challenged by intruding males, which stimulate much of the chasing that takes place over the spawning bed. When two males are attending a female, both often chase the intruder, usually abandoning pursuit when the intruder escapes into a pool next to the riffle. Once the female starts spawning, she continues the process irregularly and with different males until she is spent. When finished, the spawners return to their solitary habits.

Shorthead Redhorse, *Moxostoma macrolepidotum* (LeSueur)

Scientific name: *Moxostoma* = mouth to suck (Greek); *macrolepidotum* = large scaled (Greek).

The most widely distributed redhorse in Minnesota, the shorthead (northern) redhorse occurs in lakes, rivers, and streams throughout the state. Among Minnesota redhorses, it seems to be able to adapt to the greatest variety of habitats. It is the only redhorse that has been taken in the Lake Superior drainage in Minnesota, and it is the redhorse most commonly caught by commercial fishermen in Lake of the Woods. It ranges from Hudson Bay, west into Alberta, over much of Canada, and south over the central United States as far east as the eastern seaboard from Chesapeake to Georgia.

The closest thing to a game fish among Minnesota's suckers, the shorthead redhorse bites on baited hooks and, occasionally, on plugs and wet flies. It weighs about 2 pounds in Minnesota, fights well on light tackle, and is excellent eating when baked or smoked. Its natural diet consists mostly of small aquatic organisms, especially insect larvae.

Shorthead redhorse

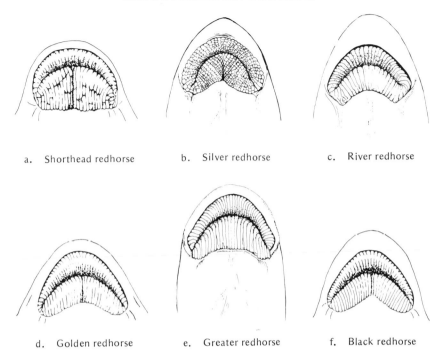

a. Shorthead redhorse   b. Silver redhorse   c. River redhorse

d. Golden redhorse   e. Greater redhorse   f. Black redhorse

Figure 43. Lips of Minnesota's redhorses: (a) the shorthead redhorse, (b) the silver redhorse, (c) the river redhorse, (d) the golden redhorse, (e) the greater redhorse, and (f) the black redhorse.

The shorthead redhorse is greenish above, golden on the sides, and white below. The scales on the back and sides have distinct dark spots at their bases. The tail fin is reddish. The head is small and conical. The mouth is also small, and the lower lips meet in a nearly straight line (Figure 43a).

The six kinds of redhorses known in Minnesota resemble each other rather closely and are sometimes confused with each other. Some species are best distinguished from each other by a combination of characteristics. The most distinctive characteristics of the shorthead redhorse are its spotted scales and the shape of its lower lips. Unfortunately, redhorses are variable. Small specimens are especially hard to identify because the characteristic colors and body proportions that help identify adults have not yet developed. As with other suckers, the safest procedure is to give the specimen to an expert for identification.

The shorthead redhorse spawns in May and June in Minnesota, most often over gravelly riffles in streams. Breeding males develop tubercles on the pelvic, anal, and tail fins. Spawning is accompanied by considerable splashing as redhorses race along the riffles with their tails flashing and their sides or backs exposed. Different species of redhorses may spawn in the same area at the same time, but they remain separate from each other.

Silver redhorse

Silver Redhorse, *Moxostoma anisurum* (Rafinesque)

Scientific name: *Moxostoma* = mouth to suck (Greek); *anisurum* = unequal tail (Greek).

Dwelling in lakes, rivers, and streams in Minnesota, the silver redhorse is known from all of the state's drainage systems except the Lake Superior drainage. Most state records are from the St. Croix and Zumbro rivers and Lake of the Woods. This fish is less common in Minnesota than the shorthead redhorse and, if previous reports of its occurrence in the state are reliable, it may be less abundant today than it was in the past. Its range is from the Hudson Bay drainage westward to Alberta and southward to Georgia.

The silver redhorse occasionally reaches a weight of as much as 8 pounds in Minnesota. It is gray or brownish above and white below. Its sides, as its common name suggests, are silvery. Its head and eyes are large. The mouth is small, and the lower lips are thin and meet at a sharp angle (Figure 43b). A helpful distinguishing characteristic is the dorsal fin, which is longer than that of other Minnesota redhorses and usually has 15 rays (with a range of 14 to 16) in comparison to the 12 to 15 of the others.

The feeding and spawning habits of the silver redhorse are similar to those of the shorthead redhorse, but it spawns a few weeks earlier than the latter species.

River Redhorse, *Moxostoma carinatum* (Cope)

Scientific name: *Moxostoma* = mouth to suck (Greek); *carinatum* = keel (Latin).

The river redhorse was not reported from Minnesota until 1968, which is remarkable considering that it reaches a weight of 15 pounds and a length of 3 feet and is locally common in two well-studied rivers, the St. Croix and the lower Mississippi. Specimens of the river redhorse have actually been taken in Minnesota in the past; they were not correctly identified, however, chiefly because the heavy and molarlike pharyngeal teeth, the most distinctive characteristic of this species, were not dissected out and examined. The pharyngeal teeth are obviously different from the comblike pharyngeal teeth of other Minnesota redhorses (Figure 44).

The river redhorse has a discontinuous distribution from Quebec southward to southern Mississippi. The main part of its range is south of Minnesota, and it extends into the state in the large, moderately clear rivers of the Mississippi system. Its former presence in the Minnesota River has been verified by examining pharyngeal teeth from specimens that were collected there in the 1890s but not correctly identified until recently. It has not been found in the Minnesota River in recent years. It is apparently also becoming rare in other parts of its range, such as Iowa, the Missouri River, the Ohio River, and the southeastern United States. Although it holds its own in clean rivers such as the St. Croix, apparently it cannot tolerate the increased pollution and siltation that has occurred in sizable portions of its river habitat during this century.

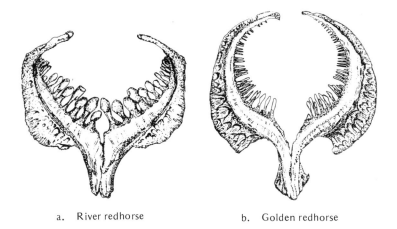

a. River redhorse   b. Golden redhorse

Figure 44. Pharyngeal teeth of (a) the river redhorse and (b) the golden redhorse.

The river redhorse is brownish above, yellowish or silvery on the sides, and white below. The scales on the back and sides have dark spots at their bases. The tail fin is reddish. The head is quite large, and the lips are thick (Figure 43c).

The diet of the river redhorse has been studied in the Cahaba River in Alabama, where it eats mostly small clams. This fish spawns in the spring over gravel in shallow areas. Males develop tubercles on their snouts and anal and tail fins and precede females onto the spawning ground. When a male sees a female approach, he attracts her with rhythmic movements, in which he is usually joined by a second male. In preparation for spawning, the two males hold the female between them and all three fish vibrate their bodies. One of the males sometimes leaves before actual spawning occurs. Eggs are shed and fertilized and settle among crevices in the gravel. The young hatch in a few days and grow rapidly.

Golden Redhorse, *Moxostoma erythrurum* (Rafinesque)

Scientific name: *Moxostoma* = mouth to suck (Greek); *erythrurum* = red tailed (Greek).

The golden redhorse lives in rivers, streams, and lakes throughout much of Minnesota except the Lake Superior drain-

Golden redhorse

age. It is locally common in the Zumbro River and in tributaries of the Minnesota. It seems to be the second most abundant redhorse in Minnesota after the shorthead redhorse. Its range is from Minnesota eastward to Lake Erie and as far south as Alabama.

The golden redhorse attains a length of about 2 feet in Minnesota. It is olive colored on top, golden on the sides, and white below. The head is moderate in size, and the eyes are small. The lower lips meet at an angle (Figure 43d). Despite its specific name of *erythrurum* (red tailed), its fins are usually dusky in color. No one characteristic readily distinguishes the golden redhorse from all other Minnesota redhorses. It is most often confused with the shorthead and silver redhorses, because these are the other redhorses most commonly associated with it. Its mouth is larger than that of the shorthead redhorse, and its lower lips meet at an angle rather than in a nearly straight line. Its dorsal fin is shorter than that of the silver redhorse and has an average of 13 rays (range 12 to 15), in contrast to the silver redhorse's average of 15 (range 14 to 16).

The golden redhorse spawns in May and June in Minnesota over riffles so shallow that the backs of the spawning fish are frequently out of the water. The golden redhorse's spawning behavior resembles that of the shorthead redhorse. Breeding males have well-developed tubercles on their anal and tail fins.

Greater Redhorse, *Moxostoma valenciennesi* Jordan

Scientific name: *Moxostoma* = mouth to suck (Greek); *valenciennesi* = named for Achille Valenciennes, a French naturalist.

Long one of Minnesota's mystery fishes, where its occurrence outside of the lower Mississippi River system was a matter of dispute, the greater redhorse has recently been found in the upper Mississippi above St. Anthony Falls in Minneapolis and in the Otter Tail River in the Red River drainage. It is not known from the Lake Superior drainage, and reports of it in Lake of the Woods await substantiation. Its range is from North Dakota through portions of the Great Lakes basin to the St. Lawrence River.

A large redhorse that attains a weight of about 10 pounds, the greater redhorse lives in clear lakes and streams and has little tolerance for pollution and siltation. It is greenish or brownish on the back, silvery or yellowish on the sides, and white below. Its head is large, and its thick lower lips meet at an angle (Figure 43e). Its fins are the most colorful of any Minnesota redhorse. The dorsal fin is gray with a distinct red band along its outer edge. All the other fins are red. The most distinctive characteristic of this redhorse is the presence of 15 or 16 scale rows around the caudal peduncle, in contrast to the average of 12 in other Minnesota redhorses.

Little is known about the habits of the greater redhorse. It is thought to eat the same kinds of immature insects and small organisms that other redhorses eat and to spawn in the spring and early summer in moderately rapid streams.

The greater redhorse is named for Achille Valenciennes (1794–1865), the well-known French naturalist who first described it.

Black Redhorse, *Moxostoma duquesnei* (LeSueur)

Scientific name: *Moxostoma* = mouth to suck (Greek); *duquesnei* = named for Fort Duquesne in Pennsylvania.

Known in Minnesota only from shallow, clean branches of the Root and Zumbro rivers in the southeastern part of the state, the black redhorse is the smallest of Minnesota's redhorses and the one most restricted in its habitat. It is intolerant of pollution and siltation. It reaches the northern limits of its range in the Mississippi River system in Minnesota and extends eastward to southern Ontario and southward to Oklahoma and Alabama.

The black redhorse occasionally exceeds 5 pounds in the South, but those taken in Minnesota, most of which were sexually mature, were 15 or fewer inches long and weighed less than a pound. The specimens that were ready to spawn were collected in May.

The black redhorse is dark olive green above, silvery on the sides, and white below. Its body is elongated and more slender than that of the other Minnesota redhorses. Its head is moderate in size, its eyes are large, and its snout protrudes down over the mouth. Its lower lips meet at an angle (Figure 43f). Whereas the other Minnesota redhorses average about 43 lateral-line scales, the black redhorse averages 45 (with a range of 44 to 48). All Minnesota redhorses typically have either 9 or 10 rays in each pelvic fin, but the black redhorse has 10 more commonly (about half the time) than the others.

A bottom feeder, the black redhorse eats a variety of small aquatic organisms and debris. Young individuals mostly eat algae. Spawning occurs in shallow, gravelly areas in streams. Breeding males develop tubercles on all fins except the dorsal fin, with those on the anal and tail fins best developed. Males establish territories and wait for females to approach. The dominant males take the choicest spots, and small males are relegated to the edges of the spawning ground. The female is usually joined by two males, who press against her from either side. The three fish vibrate their bodies until the eggs are released and fertilized. The eggs settle into crevices in the gravel on the bottom.

White Sucker, *Catostomus commersoni* (Lacépède)

Scientific name: *Catostomus* = subterminal mouth (Greek); *commersoni* = named for Philibert Commerson, a French naturalist.

The white sucker is the most common and widespread sucker in Minnesota and is among the most common fishes in the state. It is especially abundant in lakes and streams in the northern and eastern sectors. It is a widespread species that ranges from the Northwest Territories through most of Canada and as far south as New Mexico, Arkansas, Alabama, and Georgia. It is able to adapt to a wide variety of environmental conditions.

The white sucker typically attains a length of 20 inches in Minnesota and a weight of between 2 and 3 pounds, but occa-

White sucker

sionally it reaches 5 pounds. It is greenish on the back and sides and white below, but its color varies with season and time of life. Young white suckers have three distinct spots on each side, a pattern unique among Minnesota's suckers. These spots usually disappear by the time the fish reaches a length of 6 inches. A breeding male becomes distinctly blackish on its back and develops a pale reddish band along each side.

Both the white sucker and the longnose sucker can be distinguished from other Minnesota suckers by their having scales more crowded and distinctly smaller toward the front of the body than toward the rear. The white sucker can be distinguished from the longnose sucker by its having 55 to 75 lateral-line scales, in contrast to the longnose sucker's 90 or more. The white sucker could be confused with the blue sucker, but the blue sucker is an extremely rare fish in Minnesota and has more than 20 rays in the dorsal fin, in comparison to the white sucker's 11 to 13.

Young white sucker with spots on sides

Young white suckers feed on tiny organisms that they capture at or near the surface of the water. Adults are bottom feeders that consume small animals, vegetation, and ooze that is rich in nutrients. This species spawns in April and May in Minnesota. It either spawns in shallows near the edges of lakes or migrates up streams toward headwater areas or until it reaches an impassable barrier. Spawning usually takes place in shallows over rocky or gravelly bottoms. Males come to the spawning areas first. When a female enters, one or several males pursue her. As with many suckers, spawning is usually accomplished by two males and one female. Suckers produce eggs in prolific quantities, and it is not unusual for a spawning female white sucker to contain more than 100,000 eggs.

The white sucker is an important fish in Minnesota. Because of its abundance, it is a readily available source of food for game fishes. It also competes with other fishes for space and food. It does not bite on hooks often, but it is commonly netted or trapped and eaten. The flesh is bony but firm and sweet. It is usually baked, smoked, or pickled, and it can be used to make fish soup. The most important economic role of the white sucker is probably its use by the bait industry. Selling bait is a major business in Minnesota, and the white sucker seems to be the bait fish most popular with the state's anglers. The demand for white suckers for bait is so great that they are propagated in ponds to ensure that there is a ready supply. One reason for the popularity of the white sucker as a bait fish is that it gets much bigger than other good bait fishes, such as the fathead minnow. Many anglers who go after trophy walleyes, northern pike, and muskies like large, live bait fishes and use suckers as much as a foot long.

The white sucker was named for Philibert Commerson (1727–1773), a French naturalist.

Longnose Sucker, *Catostomus catostomus* (Forster)

Scientific name: *Catostomus* = subterminal mouth (Greek).

The only sucker known from both the Old and the New Worlds, the longnose sucker is a northern species that occurs in Siberia and in North America from Alaska through Canada southward as far as Maryland in the East and the Missouri and Columbia river systems in the West. It is found in the Hudson Bay and Lake Superior drainages in Minnesota, where it inhabits lakes and streams. It seems to be most common in large lakes. It is the only Minnesota sucker that lives in the depths of Lake Superior, where it is occasionally found in places as deep as 600 feet. It is usually found in shallower water, though. It sometimes congregates at the mouths of North Shore streams that empty into Lake Superior.

The longnose sucker attains a length of about 2 feet in Minnesota and is sometimes larger. It is blackish on the back and sides and white below. Breeding males have a bright red band along each side and develop tubercles on the lower fins and tail. As the common name suggests, the snout is long and extends distinctly beyond the mouth. As in the white sucker, the scales toward the front of the body are distinctly smaller and more crowded than those toward the rear. The longnose sucker has 90 or more scales in the lateral line, whereas the white sucker has only 55 to 75.

The longnose sucker spawns in May and June in Minnesota, when adults from Lake Superior migrate up the North Shore streams and adults that live inland travel into outlets between lakes. It is often accompanied on its spawning runs by the white sucker. Each spawning female is attended by two to four males, who clasp her with their pelvic fins or vibrate against her as they spawn. The longnose sucker is good to eat, especially when smoked. It is most often taken in commercial nets or by being speared as it makes its spawning runs through shallow streams.

Family ICTALURIDAE
The Catfishes

The catfishes of the family Ictaluridae are distinctive fishes well known for their broad heads, barbels (sometimes called whiskers or feelers), and smooth, scaleless skin. They have a fleshy adipose fin on the back behind the dorsal fin. This family is restricted to North America and contains 37 species, 9 of which are found in Minnesota. These 9 consist of 3 large catfishes (channel catfish, blue catfish, and flathead catfish), 3 bullheads (black bullhead, brown bullhead, and yellow bullhead), and 3 small, less well known kinds (tadpole madtom, slender madtom, and stonecat).

Catfishes are adaptable fishes that feed opportunistically on a variety of food items. They are most active at night. Spawning catfishes deposit their eggs in sheltered places or in nests they have made, and they exhibit varying degrees of care for the eggs and the young that hatch. Young bullheads remain together temporarily in schools and are attended by at least one parent as they swim about. Catfishes make excellent eating.

The name catfish comes from the long, flexible barbels, or whiskers, on the fishes' heads. These structures contain numerous taste buds and help the catfish detect food in the water. Catfishes should be handled carefully because they can "sting" with a mild venom that is released when a person's skin is punctured by a hard ray of the dorsal or pectoral fins. It is these hard rays, not the barbels, that cause the wound. The venom is most developed in the madtoms.

Minnesota's catfishes show how similar species can take advantage of the different habitats available in the environment. The large channel, the blue, and the flathead catfishes are most common in large rivers. There the flathead catfish, especially, spends much of its time in pools and backwaters, where the water moves slowly. Bullheads live in both lakes and streams, and they are often abundant in places where the water is still or sluggish and turbid and where the bottom is soft. The madtoms, which are smaller than the other catfishes, are often found in small streams. One of them, the tadpole madtom, also lives in the shallows of lakes.

Channel Catfish, *Ictalurus punctatus* (Rafinesque)

Scientific name: *Ictalurus* = fish cat (Greek);
punctatus = spotted (Latin).

The channel catfish is most common in Minnesota in the lower Mississippi and its large tributaries, such as the St. Croix,

Channel catfish

Minnesota, and Blue Earth rivers. It is also known from the Red River system and from the St. Louis River in the Lake Superior drainage. It ranges over much of the United States between the Rockies and the eastern states. The channel catfish attains a maximum weight of about 40 pounds in Minnesota. The state hook-and-line record for the fish is 38 pounds. Specimens of 3 to 5 pounds commonly are caught by anglers, who value the channel catfish for its tastiness and its fighting qualities.

Colored light olive to gray on the back and sides and whitish below, the channel catfish is marked with dark spots scattered on its back and sides. Its tail fin is deeply forked, as is that of the blue catfish. The channel catfish can be distinguished from the blue catfish by the channel catfish's dark spots (although large channel catfish darken and lose the spots) and its having fewer anal fin rays (24 to 29) than the blue catfish has (30 to 35). Both the channel catfish and the blue catfish can be distinguished from the flathead catfish by the shape of the tail fin, which is rounded in the flathead. The flathead also has a shorter anal fin (14 to 17 rays) than the others.

Confirmed catfish anglers often seek the channel catfish at night, when it forages for insects, clams, snails, small fishes, and vegetation. It can be taken on numerous kinds of bait, including worms, minnows, crayfish, and "stink" baits, such as chicken entrails. It occasionally surprises people by striking plugs and spinners. It is excellent eating when fried, baked, or smoked.

The channel catfish spawns in the late spring and early summer. Little is known of its breeding habits in Minnesota, but in other areas spawning takes place in sheltered places that the male finds and cleans ahead of time. The male then guards the nest for about two weeks until the young that hatch have left.

A valuable food and game fish in the Midwest and the South, the channel catfish is cultured in rearing ponds in some places. The Minnesota DNR has recently begun propagating this species in rearing ponds. These fish are now being distributed in southwestern Minnesota in hopes that they will provide sport and food fishing in the relatively turbid lakes and streams there, where more sensitive game fishes fail to thrive.

Blue Catfish, *Ictalurus furcatus* (LeSueur)

Scientific name: *Ictalurus* = fish cat (Greek); *furcatus* = forked (Latin).

The blue catfish lives in large rivers and is itself one of the largest of North American fishes. Several verifiable records of blue catfish weighing more than 100 pounds are known, two of them as recently as 1964 (100 pounds, Missouri River in South Dakota, and 117 pounds, Osage River in Missouri). Other reports of even larger specimens exist, including a "blue channel cat" of 315 pounds from the Missouri River near Portland, Missouri, in 1866. This species ranges over the south-central United States into Mexico and extends northward in the Missouri and Mississippi river systems.

Bluish gray on the back and sides and whitish below, the blue catfish lacks spots. It feeds on various small organisms, including immature insects, clams, snails, and crayfish. As it grows, it tends to add small fishes to its diet. It can be caught on various live and "stink" baits. Its large size and tastiness make it a valuable food fish. The blue catfish spawns in the early summer. Males select a nest site in which spawning occurs, and they guard their nests for about two weeks, by which time the young have hatched and left.

The blue catfish is considered by some to be native to Minnesota, and it may have occurred naturally in the state in the past. A few catfishes taken in Minnesota have been identified as blue catfish, but the authors know of no authenticated records. This species is somewhat migratory in the Mississippi, and the construction of dams along the river might have inhibited its northward movements in recent years.

The Minnesota DNR has recently begun stocking the blue catfish in Minnesota. In 1977, it planted 6,000 fingerlings from Alabama in Lake St. Croix. A blue catfish weighing half a pound and thought to be from this group was netted by DNR personnel in Lake Pepin the next summer. In 1979, the DNR placed 7,000 fingerlings in the hatchery at Waterville to serve as brood stock for the eventual introduction of the blue catfish into lakes and rivers in central and eastern Minnesota. If successful, this program could provide another important fish for Minnesota anglers.

Black Bullhead, *Ictalurus melas* (Rafinesque)

Scientific name: *Ictalurus* = fish cat (Greek);
melas = black (Greek).

Often found in stagnant or slow-moving water over a soft bottom, the black bullhead occurs throughout the central United States and lives in lakes and streams over much of Minnesota. It sometimes congregates in confined areas, such as below dams at the outlets of lakes. It is a hardy fish that tolerates muddy water, warm temperatures, and low oxygen availability, often living where it and other adaptable species are free from competition from more sensitive fishes that cannot withstand such conditions. Black bullheads rarely exceed 2 pounds in Minnesota, and most individuals are much smaller. This is the smallest of Minnesota's bullheads, maturing when 6 to 10 inches long.

The black bullhead is greenish brown to black above and yellowish below. Adults have a light-colored bar at the base of the tail fin. The black bullhead resembles the brown bullhead, and distinguishing the two can be difficult. Although its color is variable, the brown bullhead is often mottled brown and green above and whitish below. The barbs on the hard rays of the pectoral fins are more strongly developed in the brown bullhead (Figure 45), which also usually has 21 to 24 soft rays in the anal

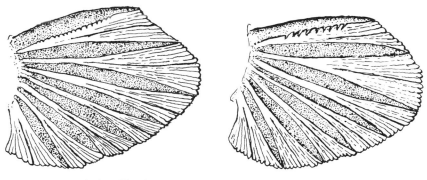

a. Black bullhead   b. Brown bullhead

Figure 45. Hard rays in pectoral fins of (a) the black bullhead and (b) the brown bullhead.

fin, compared to the black bullhead's 17 to 21. The barbels under the mouth of black and brown bullheads are black to gray, distinguishing both of these species from the yellow bullhead, which has white barbels under the mouth.

The black bullhead is a scavenger that eats just about anything digestible, including vegetation, insects, frogs, crayfish, small fishes, and other aquatic organisms. Bullheads are considered to be rough fishes, but they bite readily on worms and make excellent eating when fried or baked.

The black bullhead spawns from April through June. The spawning nest is typically in a protected place and is guarded by one parent. After the young hatch, they remain together as a group for about two weeks, during which time at least one adult accompanies and guards them. The school disperses when the young are about an inch long.

In a survey of Minnesota's Lake Minnetonka in 1949, the black and the yellow bullheads were found to be common and the brown bullhead was taken only occasionally. By the late 1960s, it was apparent that Lake Minnetonka was being polluted by excess nutrients. In a survey made in 1969, the black bullhead was abundant, the yellow bullhead was rare, and the brown bullhead was not found, suggesting that it was then rare, if not absent. This example indicates that, although the fish fauna does not necessarily diminish as the environment changes, the relative abundance of the species present does change.

Albino bullhead, *Ictalurus natalis*

Brown bullhead

Brown Bullhead, *Ictalurus nebulosus* (LeSueur)

Scientific name: *Ictalurus* = fish cat (Greek);
nebulosus = clouded (Latin).

The brown bullhead generally is common in lakes and streams throughout most of Minnesota. Large populations live in backwaters of the Mississippi, Minnesota, and St. Croix rivers and their tributaries. This species ranges over the eastern half of the United States and is known from Canada. It reaches a weight of 3 or 4 pounds but seldom gets that big.

The brown bullhead resembles the black bullhead in its habits and appearance and can best be distinguished from the black bullhead by its mottled coloration and more strongly developed barbs on the hard rays of the pectoral fins. The brown bullhead is an opportunistic feeder and is readily caught on worms.

The brown bullhead spawns from April through June in Minnesota. Spawning occurs in sheltered places or in nests fanned out in the bottom. The young that hatch remain together for about two weeks after hatching, and one or both parents remain with them and guard them until they disperse.

Yellow Bullhead, *Ictalurus natalis* (LeSueur)

Scientific name: *Ictalurus* = fish cat (Greek); *natalis* = having large buttocks (Latin).

The yellow bullhead is locally common in some of the slow streams and shallow lakes in southern Minnesota. It is less common and less widely distributed in Minnesota than the black and the brown bullheads and is not known from the northern one-third of the state. Its range is the eastern United States. It rarely exceeds 2 pounds in Minnesota, and most individuals are much smaller.

The yellow bullhead is yellowish brown to black above, with the belly yellow to white. The barbels under the mouth are white, in contrast to the black or gray barbels of the black and the brown bullheads. The yellow bullhead also has more rays in its anal fin (23 to 27) than the other two bullheads. As do other bullheads, it eats a variety of food items depending on what is available.

Yellow bullhead showing normal coloration

The yellow bullhead spawns in May and June in Minnesota and guards its eggs and the young that hatch.

Flathead Catfish, *Pylodictis olivaris* (Rafinesque)

Scientific name: *Pylodictis* = mud fish (Greek); *olivaris* = olive colored (Latin).

Like the other large species of catfishes in Minnesota, the flathead catfish is most abundant in large streams, such as the lower Mississippi, Minnesota, and St. Croix rivers. Flatheads are common in river lakes, such as Lake St. Croix and Lake Pepin, where several large specimens have been trapped recently by DNR personnel. This species is known to grow to about 100 pounds in the Missouri River system. The Minnesota hook-and-line record for flathead catfish is 70 pounds. The flathead catfish ranges over the central United States into Mexico.

In its realm of the large river, the flathead catfish seems to avoid the current most of the time by occupying specific habitats away from it. Young flatheads are often found in riffles, but there they typically lie on the substrate or among rocks. As they mature, flatheads increasingly tend to stay in pools, backwaters, and sheltered places, probably entering swift water most frequently at night while searching for food. Flatheads observed in aquariums and ponds have been observed resting on the bottom for long periods.

The typical flathead catfish is mottled brown and yellow, with its coloration becoming an increasingly uniform olive brown or grayish with age. As the common name for this species suggests, the fish's head is quite broad and flattened. In contrast to the channel catfish and the blue catfish, the flathead catfish has a protruding lower jaw that projects farther forward than the upper jaw.

The flathead catfish eats a variety of living food and carrion. Young individuals consume quantities of aquatic insects and crayfish, and small fishes are added to the diet as the flathead grows. Flatheads can be caught on live bait and "stink" bait. Spawning takes place in June and July, and the male selects a nest and guards it until the young have dispersed.

The behavior of the flathead catfish and the channel catfish in the winter in Minnesota has recently been observed for the first time. Both of these fishes expend minimal energy as they endure the cold season by lying dormant on the bottom in the shelter of rocks. Aggregations are most concentrated where rocks are abundant and the bottom is clean sand.

The Minnesota DNR has recently begun rearing flathead catfish for distribution to selected lakes.

Stonecat, *Noturus flavus* Rafinesque

Scientific name: *Noturus* = back tail (Greek), referring to the connection between the adipose fin and the tail fin; *flavus* = yellow (Latin).

Stonecats and madtoms are small, peculiar catfishes that can be distinguished by their having their adipose fins continuous with the tail fins rather than distinct from them, as they are in the large catfishes and the bullheads.

The stonecat lives in both rivers and streams in Minnesota. It seems most common in the St. Croix and in tributaries of the Mississippi and Minnesota rivers in the southern half of the state. Stonecats living in clear streams in southern Minnesota are often found in riffles, where they find refuge in crevices and under rocks. They are sometimes concentrated just below dams on streams and rivers. The stonecat ranges over the Midwest and into Canada.

The stonecat reaches a length of about 6 inches in Minnesota. It is brownish, grayish, or black above and white below. It is intermediate in stoutness between the tadpole madtom and the

Stonecat

slender madtom, and its upper jaw projects distinctly forward over the lower.

The stonecat eats a variety of small aquatic organisms and some vegetation. It spawns in the spring and, as do the madtoms, builds a nest and guards the eggs and the young. It is sometimes used as bait by anglers fishing for walleyes and large catfishes in the Mississippi in southern Minnesota.

Tadpole Madtom, *Noturus gyrinus* (Mitchill)

Scientific name: *Noturus* = back tail (Greek), referring to the connection between the adipose fin and the tail fin; *gyrinus* = tadpole (Greek).

The most common and widely distributed madtom in Minnesota, the tadpole madtom is known from all drainage systems in the state. It is the only madtom that commonly lives in lakes in Minnesota, in which it sometimes congregates in shallow, weedy places. It also lives in both turbid and clear streams, where it is most often found in quiet water over a soft bottom. It ranges from Canada through the Midwest to the southern and eastern states.

The tadpole madtom reaches a length of about 4 inches. It is yellowish gray to brown above and white below. It has a stouter body than the slender madtom and the stonecat and, indeed, does resemble a tadpole.

The tadpole madtom is a secretive fish that is most active at night, when it feeds on aquatic plants, including algae, and small aquatic animals, such as insects. It spawns in the spring and early summer, typically depositing its eggs as a mass on submerged logs, boards, or other debris. One parent remains to guard the eggs and the young.

Slender Madtom, *Noturus exilis* Nelson

Scientific name: *Noturus* = back tail (Greek), referring to the connection between the adipose fin and tail fin; *exilis* = slim (Latin).

The rarer of Minnesota's two madtoms, the slender madtom apparently is limited in the state to small, clear streams in the southeast corner. It has a comparatively limited range in the central United States. It lives in riffles or in pools and sometimes conceals itself in leaf litter in quiet places. The only verifiable record of this fish from Minnesota consists of three specimens collected by Conservation Department personnel in Otter Creek in Mower County in 1954. This species seems to reach the limits of its range in the area of southern Minnesota and is further restricted by its need for clear, flowing water.

The slender madtom varies from yellowish green to black above and is white below. It is slimmer than the tadpole madtom and the stonecat, and it has distinctly toothlike barbs on the hard rays of its pectoral fins.

The habits of the slender madtom have not been studied in Minnesota. In other places, it is known to be most active at night, when it feeds on various small organisms and vegetation. It typically deposits its eggs under a flat surface such as a rock, and one or both parents guard the eggs and the young.

Family PERCOPSIDAE
The Trout-perches

The family Percopsidae includes the trout-perches, small fishes that are so named because they have characteristics of both the trouts and the perches. They have an adipose fin, as do the

Trout-perch

trouts, but their scales are the same type as those of the perches. They are also reminiscent of the perches in that they possess spines, but these generally are weakly developed. Two species of trout-perches are living today and both are restricted to North America. One species, the trout-perch, lives in Minnesota.

Trout-perch, *Percopsis omiscomaycus* (Walbaum)

Scientific name: *Percopsis* = perchlike (Greek); *omiscomaycus* = probably an Indian name that contains the root *trout*.

The trout-perch is found over much of Minnesota in rivers and clear lakes. It is less common in small streams. Its range is from Alaska through central Canada to the middle and eastern United States.

The trout-perch seldom exceeds a length of 5 inches. It is silvery or translucent and has dark spots in a series along its back and sides. It resembles a small perch but can be distinguished from a perch by its having an adipose fin.

Trout-perch are most active at night, when they move into shallow water to feed on various small aquatic animals at or near the bottom. They stay in deeper water in the day and usually lie quietly in the concealment of debris. The trout-perch is subject to summer die-offs in Minnesota lakes such as Mille Lacs, probably due to high water temperature. Although it is of little direct economic importance, the trout-perch is useful because it is eaten by several large and important fishes, such as the walleye, northern pike, lake trout, and brook trout.

The trout-perch spawns from late spring to midsummer in Minnesota. Spawning takes place in shallow water over sand and gravel bottoms, and spawning adults sometimes move from lakes into shallow tributaries.

Family APHREDODERIDAE

The Pirate Perch

The family Aphredoderidae has only one living species, the pirate perch of the eastern United States.

Pirate Perch, *Aphredoderus sayanus* (Gilliams)

Scientific name: *Aphredoderus* = from *aphrod*, meaning excrement, and *dere*, meaning throat (Greek), referring to the location of the vent; *sayanus* = named for Thomas Say, an American naturalist.

The pirate perch reaches the northern limits of its range in the Mississippi River system of southeastern Minnesota, where it inhabits soft-bottomed sloughs, overflow ponds, and sluggish streams and backwaters. Its range includes the midwestern, southern, and eastern states.

The pirate perch attains a length of about 5 inches. It is brownish or purplish on the back and sides and white or yellowish below, though breeding males are blackish. There is a dark vertical band in front of the tail fin. The dorsal, anal, and pelvic fins have short, weakly developed spines. The most noteworthy characteristic of the pirate perch is the position of the vent, which is under the belly in the young but migrates forward to the throat as the fish grows. The pirate perch resembles a small sunfish, but its spines are much less developed. Adults can be distinguished from all other Minnesota fishes by the location of the anus.

A secretive fish, the pirate perch spends much of its time concealed in vegetation and debris. It is most active at night, when it seeks aquatic insects, crustaceans, and small fishes to eat. It spawns in the spring and is said to build a nest.

The pirate perch is named for Thomas Say (1787–1834), an

American naturalist and explorer who became a member of the utopian community at New Harmony, Indiana. The fish was first called a pirate perch by an observer who saw it eating small fishes in an aquarium.

Family GADIDAE
The Codfishes

The family Gadidae is composed mostly of ocean fishes, such as the famous codfish, haddock, and hake. Only one kind of strictly freshwater codfish, the burbot, lives in North America, and Minnesota is within its range.

Codfishes have tiny scales, a barbel on the chin, and long dorsal and anal fins. Certain codfishes are widely used as human food and as a source of cod-liver oil, which ranks them among the most important commercial fishes in the world.

Burbot, *Lota lota* (Linnaeus)

Scientific name: *Lota* = from *la lotte*, meaning codfish (French).

A northern species that is typically found in cold water, the burbot is most common in Minnesota in large, northern lakes, including Lake Superior. It also lives in rivers. Its range is from the area of the Arctic Ocean southward to the northern and central United States. The burbot is known by several names in Minnesota, including eelpout, lawyer, loche, ling, and cusk. It is also sometimes called the dogfish, just as the bowfin is.

The burbot can reach a weight of 10 pounds or more. Its back and sides are brownish and mottled with brown and black. Its belly is white. Its eyes are small and are located on top of the fish's broad head. The burbot's body is slimy and appears scaleless, though it is actually covered by tiny, embedded scales.

A secretive fish that is most active at night when it searches

Burbot

for food, the burbot eats mostly insects, crayfish, and smaller fishes. Burbots also eat the eggs of other fishes. The burbot stays in deep water most of the summer but is more active in the winter and is sometimes caught on hook and line. The city of Walker, Minnesota, recently began sponsoring an International Eelpout Festival on Leech Lake each January, complete with trophies and prizes.

Although commonly regarded as a nuisance, the burbot is actually a good food fish, with its white, firm flesh on a par with that of the northern pike and the walleye when baked, fried, or broiled. Though it is marketed commercially, it is not very popular in Minnesota, where more attractive food fishes are abundant. The repulsive-looking burbot might, however, become much more important in the future. As is typical of codfishes, it has a large, oily liver. The liver oil is a remarkable fluid that is rich in vitamins A and D and even has healing properties when applied to sores. The burbot's liver oil is being studied and may eventually become an important source of cod-liver oil and an ingredient in ointments. The liver residue from which oil has been extracted might also be useful as fertilizer when it is mixed with other by-products from the fish. Even the skin might be useful in the making of glue. The potential versatility of the burbot as a source of food, vitamins, fertilizer, and other products could soon cause attitudes about its usefulness to change dramatically.

The burbot is most unusual among Minnesota fishes in that it spawns in the middle of the winter. Spawning occurs in shallow water in lakes and small streams. Females produce eggs in great quantities and shed them randomly over the substrate. Spawning adults are known to gather together in writhing masses.

Family CYPRINODONTIDAE
The Killifishes

The family Cyprinodontidae is a large group that is most successful in tropical areas. This family decreases in abundance and diversity in the north, with only two kinds, the banded killifish and the plains topminnow, known from Minnesota. Killifishes live in both fresh and brackish water, and some species are common around the mouths of rivers and in the shallow waters of the Gulf of Mexico. Some species live in isolated springs in desert areas in the southwestern United States.

Killifishes are small, colorful fishes in which the dorsal fin is set far back over the anal fin, the tail fin is rounded, and spines are absent. Members of this family are sometimes called topminnows because they feed on insects and other small animals while skimming along just below the surface of the water. Killifishes are well adapted for this method of feeding, with their heads flattened on top, their mouths tilted upward, and their lower jaws protruding. Because they eat organisms such as larval mosquitoes, killifishes are useful in helping to control insects. They die too quickly in bait buckets to be good bait fishes.

Banded Killifish, *Fundulus diaphanus* (LeSueur)

Scientific name: *Fundulus* = from *fundus,* meaning bottom (Latin); *diaphanus* = transparent (Greek).

The banded killifish lives in lakes and streams over most of Minnesota, except in the cold streams and lakes in the northeastern portion of the state. It seems to be most common in lakes in the central and southern parts of the state, where it is found in shallow, weedy water over sandy bottoms. It can become

Banded killifish

abundant in lakes where it finds favorable surroundings, such as Lake Minnetonka. It ranges from southern Canada through eastern North Dakota, Minnesota, and Iowa and to the mideastern United States as far south and east as South Carolina.

The banded killifish is usually less than 4 inches long. It is greenish above and silvery to whitish on the sides and belly. As its common name suggests, it has blackish vertical bands (usually 14 to 16 in number) on its sides. Colors are brightest in breeding season, especially in males. Breeding males often develop two blackish stripes on the dorsal fin. The plains topminnow, which is the closest relative of the banded killifish in Minnesota, is plainer in color and lacks the vertical bands. The banded killifish also has smaller scales (more than 40 in a lengthwise series along the side) than the plains topminnow (33 to 36). Killifishes resemble other small fishes such as minnows, but they can be distinguished by their flattened heads, tilted mouths, and protruding lower jaws.

The banded killifish eats mostly insects and other small aquatic animals. Apparently, it spawns throughout much of the summer in Minnesota, with the females depositing their eggs at random over sand and weeds in shallow water.

Plains Topminnow, *Fundulus sciadicus* Cope

Scientific name: *Fundulus* = from *fundus*, meaning bottom (Latin); *sciadicus* = a kind of dusky fish (Greek).

The plains topminnow has been found in only two places in Minnesota, the Kanaranzi Creek in Rock County and the Rock

River in Pipestone County. Both of these streams are tributaries of the Missouri River in the extreme southwestern corner of the state. The plains topminnow has a rather unusual and limited range that centers on the Missouri River system from eastern Wyoming to southwestern Minnesota and northwestern Iowa. Two isolated populations occur to the south, one in central Missouri and a second in the area where Missouri, Kansas, and Oklahoma border each other.

A small fish typically less than 3 inches long, the plains topminnow is most often found in clear, quiet pools and backwaters over submerged vegetation. It is greenish to brownish above and white below. It is rather drab in color, although the pale yellow fins brighten to orange in breeding males. It can be distinguished from the banded killifish by the absence of distinct bands on its sides and by its larger scales. The plains topminnow has not been studied in Minnesota. Studies elsewhere show that it spawns in the summer and that females deposit their eggs on aquatic vegetation.

Family ATHERINIDAE
The Silversides

The family Atherinidae includes about 170 species of fishes called silversides. Most members of this family live in the tropics or the subtropics, and many kinds live in the sea or in coastal

Brook silverside

waters. Only one species, the brook silverside, lives in Minnesota. Silversides are related to the famous flying fishes of the ocean.

Brook Silverside, *Labidesthes sicculus* (Cope)

Scientific name: *Labidesthes* = forceps to eat (Greek), referring to the long jaws; *sicculus* = from *siccus*, meaning dried (Latin), referring to dried pools.

The brook silverside lives in clear, weedy lakes and large streams in central and southern Minnesota. Its range is from the St. Lawrence drainage west into Minnesota and south to the Gulf of Mexico.

Slender and streamlined, with a pointed snout and long, beaklike jaws, the brook silverside typically attains a length of about 4 inches. It is yellow green and silvery above and silvery white below. It gets its common name from the silvery stripes on its sides. It has two dorsal fins, the first of which contains short, flexible spines. Both the rear dorsal fin and the anal fin have a flexible spine followed by a series of soft rays. The presence of two dorsal fins and beaklike jaws distinguishes the brook silverside from other small, slim fishes, such as darters and shiners.

A schooling fish that usually swims near the surface of the water, the brook silverside eats various tiny, floating animals and sometimes leaps out of the water to catch flying insects. It is much more active in the daytime than at night.

The brook silverside spawns in the spring and early summer in Minnesota, typically in shallow, weedy water. Males pursue females almost continuously for a few days before spawning actually takes place. Eggs are shed and fertilized as spawning pairs glide from the top toward the bottom. The eggs hatch in about a week. Newly hatched young form schools and go to deep, open water until late summer, when they return to the shallows. They grow quite rapidly, reaching their maximum size before the end of the same calendar in which they hatched. They spawn the next year, and most individuals die by the end of their second summer.

Family GASTEROSTEIDAE
The Sticklebacks

The family Gasterosteidae includes the sticklebacks. These small fishes have well-developed spines, large heads, and large eyes. The body of a stickleback is scaleless and is either smooth or armed with plates. The name stickleback refers to a series of spines on the fish's back. These spines, which form part of the dorsal fin, are separate from each other and each has its own small membrane. A soft dorsal fin follows the spines.

About 10 species of sticklebacks are living today, and 2 of these, the brook stickleback and the ninespine stickleback, are found in Minnesota. Most sticklebacks live in coastal sea waters, and some move rather freely between salt and fresh water.

Brook stickleback

Brook Stickleback, *Culaea inconstans* (Kirtland)

Scientific name: *Culaea* = a name coined for this fish; *inconstans* = variable (Latin).

The only stickleback essentially confined to fresh water, the brook stickleback occurs from the Northwest Territories to Nova

Scotia and south as far as Iowa. It is found in northeastern New Mexico, well outside of its main range, where it was probably introduced along with bait minnows. It prefers cool, clear, weedy streams and ponds and is found in such habitats throughout Minnesota.

Rarely exceeding a length of 3 inches, the brook stickleback is generally greenish above and pale below. Spawning males may become partly reddish or blackish, and spawning females may become mottled. Five dorsal spines are typically present, but the number varies from three to seven (hence the specific name *inconstans*). The anal fin has a stout spine at its front, and each pelvic fin also has a stout spine. At first glance, the pelvic fins seem to consist of a spine only, because the one or two soft rays present are tiny. The body is compressed, and the caudal peduncle is distinctly slender. The tail fin is rounded. Stickle-backs can be distinguished from other Minnesota fishes by their separate dorsal spines. Whereas the brook stickleback usually has five of these spines, the ninespine stickleback, as its name suggests, usually has nine.

The brook stickleback is carnivorous, eating all manner of small aquatic animals, including small fishes and fish eggs. It also eats algae.

Sticklebacks are nest-building fishes whose fascinating breeding behavior can easily be observed in an aquarium. The brook stickleback spawns in the early summer in Minnesota. Prior to spawning, males establish territories in shallow water and each builds a nest from algae, sticks, and fragments of plants. The male uses his mouth and snout to shape the nest, which is usually a hollow globe of from 1 to 2 inches in diameter, with one opening. The male glues the nest together with a white, sticky secretion formed in his kidneys. He delivers this secretion by touching his urogenital area to the nest. The nest is usually attached to an aquatic plant just above the bottom, but some-times it is built on the bottom itself.

When a female enters his territory, the male usually strikes her one or more times with his head before swimming to the nest in an attempt to lead her there. When a female enters the nest, the male quivers against her, inducing her to shed about 50 to 100 eggs. The female then leaves the nest, typically by forcing her way out the end opposite the opening. The male fertilizes the eggs and then chases the female away. He remains to guard and fan the nest and often repairs the hole created by the female. The eggs hatch in about a week, and the male remains with the young, shepherding them until they become so active that he cannot prevent them from straying. A male often fertilizes the eggs of more than one female in a breeding season.

Ninespine Stickleback, *Pungitius pungitius* (Linnaeus)

Scientific name: *Pungitius* = pricking (Latin).

The ninespine stickleback lives in fresh water and in coastal areas of seas in northern North America, Europe, and Asia. It occurs from Alaska through Canada to the Great Lakes drainage and New Jersey. It is locally common in northern Minnesota in the Rainy River and its tributaries and in North Shore streams. It is known from Lake Winnibigoshish in the upper Mississippi River system, where it may have been introduced.

The ninespine stickleback seldom grows to be as much as 3 inches long. It is green or gray above, with irregular blotches, and silvery below. Breeding males may be reddish or blackish. As its common name suggests, the ninespine stickleback typically has nine separate dorsal spines, in contrast to the brook stickleback's five. A stout spine is found in the anal fin and in each pelvic fin. The caudal peduncle is quite slender and may have a keel on each side.

The ninespine stickleback is an aggressive little fish that resembles the brook stickleback in diet and behavior. It spawns in the summer and, despite its tolerance for salt water, is only known to spawn in fresh water. Males establish territories and build nests of plant fragments, rootlets, and algae. The nest varies in shape and is either built above the bottom amid vegetation in weedy habitats or among rocks in rocky places where vegetation is sparse. When a female approaches, the male swims toward her and then attempts to entice her to follow him to the nest by swimming toward it. The male may perform a series of movements described as the zigzag dance as he courts the female. The female deposits about 20 or 30 eggs in the nest.

The male fertilizes the eggs, chases the female away, and remains on guard.

In Canada, it has been shown that the ninespine stickleback, when abundant, is an important source of food for the walleye, lake trout, brook trout, and grayling.

Family COTTIDAE
The Sculpins

The family Cottidae includes the sculpins, peculiar-looking fishes that have broad, flattened heads and tapering bodies. Most of the 300 or so living species are marine, and the family is widely distributed in the seas of the Northern Hemisphere. Four species live in Minnesota. With their large heads, wide mouths, protruding eyes, spines on each cheek, large, fanlike pectoral fins, and slimy skin that is scaleless but that may contain prickles, Minnesota's sculpins are distinctive and rather amusing to look at. Some sculpins live in trout streams and are blamed for eating trout eggs. They have been reported to do so on occasion, but no evidence exists to show that trout eggs are a significant part of their diet.

Deepwater Sculpin, *Myoxocephalus thompsoni* (Girard)

Scientific name: *Myoxocephalus* = head resembling that of a dormouse (Greek); *thompsoni* = named for Rev. Zadock Thompson, who wrote a history of Vermont.

The deepwater sculpin exists in two forms: one lives in the Arctic Ocean and its coastal waters, and the other lives in fresh water in Asia, Europe, and North America. In North America, the freshwater form occurs as far south as the Great Lakes. The freshwater variety actually lives at greater depths than the marine form, and in Minnesota it is most often found in Lake Superior at a depth of about 600 feet. Most early records of this sculpin from Minnesota are based on specimens taken from the stomachs of lake trout and siscowets caught deep in Lake Superior. It has also been reported in a few North Shore streams.

The deepwater sculpin has four sharp, conspicuous spines on each side of its head. It attains a length of about 5 inches. It is tan on the back and sides, with dark bands, and whitish below. As do the other Minnesota sculpins, the deepwater sculpin has two dorsal fins, but these are distinctly separate in the deepwater sculpin and barely separate in the others.

Little is known of the habits of the deepwater sculpin. It eats tiny shrimplike animals and immature forms of insects that it finds on the bottom at great depths. It apparently spawns in the summer in Lake Superior.

Mottled Sculpin, *Cottus bairdi* Girard

Scientific name: *Cottus* = an old name for a European fish, the miller's thumb; *bairdi* = named for Spencer F. Baird, the first United States fish commissioner.

The mottled sculpin is the most common sculpin in Minnesota, where it lives in small streams over much of the state. Commonly, it finds shelter among rocks and debris on the bottom of riffles. Its main range is from Labrador south to Alabama, but it also occurs in the Ozark region and from Alberta through Utah in the West.

The mottled sculpin attains a length of about 5 inches. It is mottled brown on the back and sides and speckled white below. Breeding males are darker and are greenish underneath. This fish is quite similar to the slimy sculpin but usually has four rays in each pelvic fin (Figure 46a), in contrast to the slimy sculpin's three (both species have one spine in each pelvic fin, which when counting one must be sure not to confuse with a soft ray).

The mottled sculpin is a bottom dweller that eats vegetation and a variety of small aquatic animals, such as immature insects, worms, crustaceans, and small fishes. It lives in trout streams and is sometimes found in the same places as the brook trout.

The mottled sculpin apparently spawns in the spring in the Minnesota region. The male cleans out a nesting area under a rock, ledge, or tree root and entices females to enter. Females

Mottled sculpin

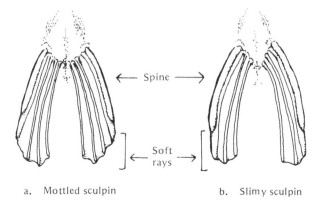

← Spine →

← Soft rays →

a. Mottled sculpin   b. Slimy sculpin

Figure 46. Pelvic fins of (a) the mottled sculpin and (b) the slimy sculpin.

turn upside down and deposit the sticky eggs on the undersurface of the top of the nest. After she spawns, the female leaves or is driven away by the male. Depending on the temperature, the eggs can take as long as a month to hatch. The male remains to guard and maintain the nest site until the young have left. Males have been observed guarding nests in February in the Ozarks.

The mottled sculpin is named for Spencer F. Baird (1823–1887), the first head of the United States Fish Commission.

Slimy Sculpin, *Cottus cognatus* Richardson

Scientific name: *Cottus* = an old name for a European fish, the miller's thumb; *cognatus* = kindred (Latin), referring to its relationship to a similar fish, *Cottus gobio*, of Europe.

The slimy sculpin is common in Minnesota in the shallow waters of Lake Superior and in North Shore streams. It is also locally common in tributaries of the St. Croix River and in streams in the southeastern part of the state. It lives in trout streams, sometimes in association with the brook trout. The slimy sculpin is known from northeastern Siberia and throughout much of northern North America from Alaska to Virginia.

A mottled brown fish that attains a length of about 5 inches, the slimy sculpin closely resembles the mottled sculpin in appearance, feeding habits, and breeding behavior. It usually has three soft rays in each pelvic fin, in contrast to the mottled sculpin's four. When the slimy sculpin and mottled sculpin are living in the same streams, the former is usually in the headwaters and the latter usually is downstream. Thus, competition between these two similar fishes is decreased.

Spoonhead Sculpin, *Cottus ricei* (Nelson)

Scientific name: *Cottus* = an old name for a European fish, the miller's thumb; *ricei* = named for M. L. Rice, who discovered it.

The spoonhead sculpin is known in Minnesota from Lake Superior and the North Shore. Its range is from the Yukon through central Canada and the Great Lakes basin. It is generally found in shallower water than the deepwater sculpin.

Slightly smaller than other Minnesota sculpins, the spoonhead sculpin seldom exceeds 4 inches in length. It is mottled brown on the back and sides and white below. Its head is distinctly flattened, and its eyes are perched on top. The skin is typically sprinkled with tiny prickles, which one can feel by running a finger over them.

Little is known about the habits of the spoonhead sculpin. Presumably, it feeds on small aquatic animals at or near the bottom. Observations in Canada suggest that it spawns in the summer or early autumn.

Family PERCICHTHYIDAE
The Temperate Basses

The family Percichthyidae includes about 40 kinds of fishes, most of which live in the sea. This family was, in fact, only recently separated from the sea bass family, called the Serranidae. Two kinds of temperate basses, the white bass and the yellow bass, live only in fresh water, and both of them are found in Minnesota. They are both good sport fishes, although they are rather small. The Minnesota DNR has been attempting to introduce a third temperate bass, the striped bass, which is native to coastal areas of the United States and gets much bigger than the white bass and the yellow bass. The attempts have been unsuccessful so far.

Temperate basses are handsome, spiny-rayed fishes whose pelvic fins are far forward. The Minnesota species resemble crappies and the so-called largemouth and smallmouth basses of the family Centrarchidae, although the two families are not closely related. (The family Centrarchidae is the sunfish family and does not contain true basses. The authors doubt, though, that Minnesota bass anglers are about to start calling the largemouth a largemouth sunfish!) Minnesota's temperate basses can be distinguished from members of the sunfish family by the presence of a series of distinct, longitudinal stripes along their sides, dorsal fins that are almost or completely separate from each other, and a sharp spine near the rear edge of the gill cover. The most interesting difference between the temperate basses and the sunfishes, however, is behavioral. Most sunfishes have elaborate patterns of behavior related to reproduction, such as establishing territories, excavating nests for spawning, courtship, and nest guarding; the temperate basses spawn in schools in open water, with the eggs shed randomly and left to sink to the bottom to develop without attention from the parents.

White Bass, *Morone chrysops* (Rafinesque)

Scientific name: *Morone* = (meaning unknown); *chrysops* = golden eye (Greek).

The range of the white bass is from the St. Lawrence River basin westward to South Dakota and southward in the Ohio and Mississippi river systems to the Gulf of Mexico. In Minnesota, it is found in the Mississippi, Minnesota, and St. Croix river systems in the southern part of the state. Its preferred habitat is large rivers, lakes, and reservoirs in which the water is clear and the bottom is sandy or rocky.

An active, schooling fish that seldom exceeds 3 pounds in Minnesota, the white bass is silvery, with dark stripes on its sides. Both the white bass and the yellow bass resemble certain members of the sunfish family found in Minnesota, but the basses can be distinguished from the sunfishes by the longitudinal stripes on the basses' sides. The stripes are usually continuous in the white bass and discontinuous above the anal fin in the yellow bass. In the white bass, the two dorsal fins are separate from each other and the anal fin has 11 or 12 soft rays. In the yellow bass, the two dorsal fins are slightly connected and the anal fin has 9 or 10 (usually 10) soft rays.

Schools of white bass feed most actively in the early morning and late evening on small fishes, crustaceans, and insects. Feeding can become frenzied as the bass drive small fishes to the

White bass

surface and consume them. The gizzard shad is an important source of food for the white bass in Lake Pepin and Lake St. Croix.

The habit of schooling and the readiness with which white bass bite on all manner of baits such as minnows, small plugs, spinners, and flies makes this fish fun and easy to catch. The angler who fishes a school of feeding white bass is rewarded with a scrappy fighter on the end of the line at almost every cast. Despite its sporting qualities, the white bass is not sought intensively by Minnesota's anglers, perhaps because it is smaller than many of the popular game fishes. It also lacks a reputation as being delicious eating, but experienced white bass anglers say that placing the fish in a cooler after catching it, rather than on a stringer, makes for a meal suitable for the most discriminating palate.

A spring spawner in Minnesota, the white bass migrates from large rivers into tributaries and lakes, sometimes traveling considerable distances. Prior to spawning, schools of males separate from schools of females, with the males moving to the spawning grounds first. Once spawning starts, it occurs in open water over gravelly bottoms, with eggs shed, fertilized, and left to settle to the bottom to develop without parental care. The eggs hatch very soon, in about two days. One female can produce nearly a million eggs in one season.

Yellow Bass, *Morone mississippiensis* Jordan and Eigenmann

Scientific name: *Morone* = (meaning unknown); *mississippiensis* = named for the Mississippi River.

A fish distributed farther south than the white bass, the' yellow bass occurs from southern Minnesota to the Gulf of Mexico in the Mississippi River system. It is less common and widespread in Minnesota than the white bass, occurring in the state in the lower Mississippi and its backwaters, generally from Lake Pepin southward.

Similar to the white bass in size, habitat preference, and behavior, the yellow bass is a good sport fish that is of limited importance in Minnesota because of its limited distribution and lack of abundance. It resembles the white bass but is, as its common name suggests, typically more yellowish. Its longitudinal stripes are thicker than those of the white bass and typically are discontinuous above the anal fin.

The yellow bass is a schooling fish that feeds on small fishes, crustaceans, and insects. It is easily caught by casting with a variety of baits. As does the white bass, it migrates into tributaries and lakes in the spring to spawn. Eggs are shed and fertilized in open water over gravelly bottoms. The eggs settle to the bottom, where they are left unattended, and hatch in four days to a week.

Family CENTRARCHIDAE
The Sunfishes

The family Centrarchidae is among the most important of Minnesota's fish families because it includes panfishes and game fishes that provide considerable sport and food for the angler. This North American family includes 30 species, 11 of which are known from Minnesota. Sunfishes have deep, laterally flattened bodies and spines in their fins. Their pelvic fins are located beneath the pectoral fins.

The sunfishes are most abundant in fertile lakes in Minnesota, although they also occur in rivers and streams. In Minnesota and elsewhere, some kinds of sunfishes have been introduced into new habitats to the extent that their natural distribution patterns have been obscured.

Sunfishes are predaceous fishes that usually locate their food by sight. They are popular sport fishes that can be taken on worms, minnows, plugs, spinners, and artificial flies. Pound for pound, they are among the best fighting fishes.

Sunfishes have some interesting behavioral traits. They have a homing sense and often spend their lives in a specific area. If removed and released elsewhere, they find their way back. Most sunfishes make spawning nests in shallow water. The nest is a depression that is cleared by the male, who fans away bottom sediments by using his tail. Females come to the nest on their own or with the male as an escort. After spawning, the male remains and fiercely guards the eggs and the young that hatch. Sunfishes, especially the males, are more brightly colored in breeding season than at other times.

Female sunfishes sometimes deposit their eggs in the nests of other species, and hybridization sometimes results. The green sunfish, the bluegill, and the pumpkinseed hybridize most often in Minnesota. Hybrids are intermediate in appearance between the parent species but typically grow faster and to a larger size, a situation that pays dividends to anglers.

When not controlled by environmental resistance factors such as predators, sunfishes are known to overpopulate ponds and small lakes to the degree that the members of the population do not attain their normal growth and stunting results.

Largemouth Bass, *Micropterus salmoides* (Lacépède)

Scientific name: *Micropterus* = small fin (Greek), referring to a damaged dorsal fin in the specimen for which the genus was named, which made it appear as though a small fin followed the dorsal fin; *salmoides* = from *Salmo*, a Latin name for salmon.

The largemouth (black) bass is common in lakes and streams over much of Minnesota, especially in the small- and medium-size lakes in the central and north-central portions that are characterized by clear water, sandy shorelines, and weed beds. It is also locally common in relatively muddy lakes in the southern part of the state and in backwaters along the Mississippi and St. Croix rivers. It occurs in a few lakes in the Lake Superior drainage, perhaps mostly as a result of being introduced, but it is uncommon there. The largemouth occurs naturally from Canada southward over much of the eastern United States and has been introduced elsewhere. The world hook-and-line record for a largemouth is a specimen weighing 22 pounds, 4 ounces, caught in Montgomery Lake in Georgia in 1932. The Minnesota record is 10 pounds, 2 ounces.

The color of the largemouth bass varies with age and habitat. It is typically green above and white below. The young have a

Young largemouth bass

Largemouth bass

distinct black stripe along the sides of the body that usually fades with age. As its common name suggests, the largemouth bass has a relatively large mouth that usually extends behind the eye in adults. The smallmouth bass has a smaller mouth that does not extend behind the eye. In the largemouth, the spiny, front portion of the dorsal fin is separated from the soft-rayed, back portion by a relatively deep notch. The spiny portion of the dorsal fin in the smallmouth has a lower contour, and the notch that joins it to the back portion is less obvious.

Carnivorous throughout its life, the largemouth eats various small aquatic animals when it is young and consumes mostly small fishes, crayfish, frogs, and insects when it is mature. It feeds most actively in the morning and evening. It is a popular game fish, and, although the smallmouth has the reputation of being the better fighter, the largemouth is certainly not far behind it. The largemouth bass is commonly caught by casting with plugs, spinners, or minnows around lily pads and stumps near the shorelines of lakes. An especially enjoyable technique is popping for this bass by using surface plugs and then watching the fish strike.

The largemouth spawns from May to July in Minnesota. Water temperature is critical to the timing and success of spawning, which occurs after the water temperature rises to 60° F. Eggs and young die when the temprature drops suddenly by 10° F or more. Spawning usually takes place in shallow, quiet water, such as near the shorelines of lakes. The largemouth generally makes a nest in the form of a depression in the bottom that is fanned out by the male, but the female deposits eggs over vegetation or among roots if good nest sites are not at hand. Females visit nests to spawn and then leave the duty of guarding them to the males. Largemouths build their nests 30 feet or more apart, and each male guards the territory around his nest, driving away intruders. The eggs hatch in about a week, and the young form a school that remains together for as long as another month. The male parent accompanies them until they disperse.

Neither the largemouth nor the smallmouth bass responds well to artificial fertilization and modern rearing techniques, so they are not propagated by the Minnesota DNR as frequently as are walleyes and northerns. They are sometimes propagated in ponds, in which adults are allowed to make nests and fertilize the eggs. Because these basses need to establish territories between nests, relatively few nests can be built in each pond. Also, the young must be removed shortly after they hatch to prevent the adults from eating them. In managing basses, the DNR concentrates on protecting their spawning beds and timing bass fishing season to ensure maximum hatching success.

Smallmouth bass

Smallmouth Bass, *Micropterus dolomieui* Lacépède

Scientific name: *Micropterus* = small fin (Greek), referring to a damaged dorsal fin in the specimen for which the genus was named, which made it appear as though a small fin followed the dorsal fin; *dolomieui* = named for Dieudonné de Dolomieu, a French geologist.

An attractive fish and an explosive fighter, the smallmouth bass is an important game fish in Minnesota's lakes and streams. It prefers clear, moderately cold, and swift-flowing streams, such as the St. Croix River and its large tributaries. It is common in the Rum River, the Mississippi River north of St. Anthony Falls, and tributaries of the Minnesota River and in the Cannon, Zumbro, and Root rivers in southeastern Minnesota. The smallmouth was introduced accidentally into the Rainy River at the turn of this century and has migrated widely so that today almost every lake in the Boundary Waters Canoe Area has a population. Where once it was exotic, it now ranks with the northern pike and the walleye as an attraction for the angler. The smallmouth ranges naturally from southern Canada over the central and mideastern United States.

The smallmouth is generally smaller than its close relative, the largemouth, rarely exceeding 4 pounds in Minnesota. The state hook-and-line record for a smallmouth bass is 8 pounds, and the world record is 11 pounds, 15 ounces, for a specimen caught in Dale Hollow Lake, Kentucky, in 1955.

The smallmouth has a smaller mouth than the largemouth, with the mouth not extending behind the eye. Young smallmouths have vertical bars or spots on their sides and lack the black lateral bands of young largemouths. Adult smallmouths may also have vertical bars, which vary in color from dark green to pale olive brown. The markings and coloration fade quickly after the fish is caught. The eyes are more or less reddish.

The smallmouth spawns in the late spring when water temperatures reach 60° F to 65° F. Males establish territories, build nests, and guard the eggs and the young from other fishes. During this time, the male is extremely vulnerable because he will attack anything intruding on his territory — another fish, a lure, or even a swimmer or a scuba diver.

The smallmouth is a tremendous fighter and a worthy rival for the largemouth and the northern pike for the title of top Minnesota warm-water sport fish. It feeds on crayfish, small fishes, and emerging insects, such as mayflies, midges, caddisflies, and stoneflies. Spinners, small surface plugs, artificial flies, and popping lures are equally attractive to feeding smallmouths. Of course, live baits such as minnows, crayfish, worms, and insect larvae are also productive. At times, for reasons yet unknown, largemouth and smallmouth basses go on feeding sprees and take almost anything the angler has to offer. At other times, in the same area, they simply ignore the tastiest of baits and the most artfully presented lures.

The smallmouth bass was named for Dieudonné de Dolomieu (1750–1801), a French geologist for whom the mineral dolomite was also named.

Rock Bass, *Ambloplites rupestris* (Rafinesque)

Scientific name: *Ambloplites* = blunt armature (Greek); *rupestris* = living among the rocks (Latin).

An attractive, heavy-bodied sunfish, the rock bass is found in lakes and streams throughout much of Minnesota. It is likely to be common in shallow, weedy places in lakes and in lakes and streams that have soft bottoms. It ranges from southern Canada through the Midwest to the Gulf of Mexico.

The rock bass reaches a size of 10 inches in Minnesota. It is brassy in color and is marked with small but distinct black spots. It can change its pigmentation in a matter of minutes and so can adjust rapidly to the color of its immediate surroundings. It has a distinctly reddish eye, and it is sometimes known by the common name of goggle-eye in the South. It has six spines in its anal fin, distinguishing it from similar panfishes such as the warmouth, the bluegill, the pumpkinseed, and the orangespotted sunfish, all of which have three spines.

The rock bass often travels in schools and is typically found in weedy places and around submerged logs in lakes. It is an aggressive feeder that eats mostly insects, snails, and small

Rock bass

fishes. It bites readily on worms and grasshoppers and will also take small plugs, spinners, and artificial flies. The rock bass and other panfishes such as the bluegill and the pumpkinseed are especially popular with young anglers because they bite readily on live bait and can be caught by still fishing with inexpensive tackle from the shore or from a dock.

The rock bass spawns in May and June in Minnesota. The male clears out a depression in gravel on the bottom for a nest. The female comes in to spawn and leaves the male to guard the nest, which he does until the young disperse.

Warmouth, *Lepomis gulosus* (Cuvier)

Scientific name: *Lepomis* = scaled gill cover (Greek); *gulosus* = large mouthed (Latin).

The warmouth has been taken in Minnesota only in the sloughs and backwaters of the Mississippi River in the southeastern part of the state, where it reaches the northern limits of its range. It lives in sluggish, weedy, shallow water over a soft bottom. The weedy, soft-bottomed sloughs that it inhabits are difficult places in which to collect fishes, and at present it is not even certain whether the warmouth is rare in Minnesota or whether it is common in its habitat there. The warmouth occupies lowland areas over the central and southeastern states and the eastern seaboard.

The warmouth reaches a size of about 8 inches in Minnesota. It is greenish to gray above, with dark mottlings, and is yellowish below. Its upper scales each bear a black spot. It resembles the rock bass, from which it can be distinguished by its having only three spines in the anal fin, by its having a patch of small teeth on the top of the tongue, and by its having distinctly dark streaks radiating onto the operculum from the rear of the eye.

Little is known of the habits of the warmouth in Minnesota. Its life history has been studied in other places in the Midwest, where it resembles the rock bass and other sunfishes in its feeding, spawning, and social behavior.

Green Sunfish, *Lepomis cyanellus* Rafinesque

Scientific name: *Lepomis* = scaled gill cover (Greek); *cyanellus* = blue (Greek).

The green sunfish lives in lakes and streams over much of Minnesota, showing a peculiar tendency to be quite abundant in some lakes and seemingly absent from others, often even those close to each other. It is common in shallow, weedy lakes and backwaters, and it may be the most common sunfish in Minnesota's streams. It ranges from southern Canada through the Midwest into Mexico.

A colorful little fish, the green sunfish is bluish green on the back and sides, with yellow-flecked scales, and yellowish below. Its mouth is large, its pectoral fins are short and rounded, and it has a dark spot near the back of the dorsal fin. It and the other small sunfishes resemble each other but can be distinguished from one another by such characteristics as coloration, shape of pectoral fins, and size of mouth. Telling them apart is complicated by the hybridizing that they do, because the hybrids are intermediate in appearance between the parent species and have characteristics that resemble both. The most common hybrid combinations in Minnesota are green sunfish with bluegill, green sunfish with pumpkinseed, and bluegill with pumpkinseed.

The green sunfish feeds voraciously on small aquatic animals, chiefly insects. It seldom exceeds 5 inches in Minnesota, where

Green sunfish

it is smaller than it is farther south in its range. Because it nibbles the bait from anglers' hooks and is seldom large enough to be worth keeping when caught, it is generally a nuisance to the angler.

In Minnesota, the green sunfish spawns in the early summer and sometimes again in July. Males clear depressions in the bottom for nests and remain on guard after spawning is over. Whereas the largemouth and smallmouth basses are solitary nesters that require large territories, sunfishes such as the green sunfish, the bluegill, and the pumpkinseed often make their nests close together and more than one species can spawn in the same small area. Female green sunfish tend to deposit eggs in more than one nest without paying particular attention to whether the male on a given nest is another green sunfish or a different kind. This behavior leads to the hybridization that occurs among sunfishes. In some populations, hybrids are as common as the parent species. The hybrids are hardy and survive well when the oxygen content of the water is low.

Orangespotted sunfish

Orangespotted Sunfish, *Lepomis humilis* (Girard)

Scientific name: *Lepomis* = scaled gill cover (Greek); *humilis* = humble (Latin).

The orangespotted sunfish lives in the western and southern portions of Minnesota and seems most common in backwater areas of tributaries of the Minnesota and lower Mississippi rivers and in shallow lakes in the south-central part of the state. It ranges from North Dakota southward through the Midwest to the Gulf of Mexico.

The orangespotted sunfish is the smallest sunfish in Minnesota and is usually only 2 or 3 inches long. It is a colorful little fish, with its iridescent bluish head and back, orange breast and fins, and scattered orange spots on its scales. The colors are especially bright in breeding males. The pectoral fins are long and pointed, and the dorsal fin lacks a dark spot near its rear margin.

The orangespotted sunfish feeds mostly on insects and other small aquatic animals. It is of no real use as a panfish because it is so small. It spawns over nests at close quarters with other sunfishes and apparently hybridizes occasionally.

Bluegill, *Lepomis macrochirus* Rafinesque

Scientific name: *Lepomis* = scaled gill cover (Greek); *macrochirus* = large hand (Greek), possibly referring to the body shape.

The bluegill is perhaps the best-known, most common, and most popular panfish in Minnesota. It is abundant in lakes over

Bluegill sunfish

most of the state except in the northeast portion, probably because the lakes there are too cold for it. Apparently, it was
introduced into some of the northeastern lakes in which it
occurs today. It also lives in rivers and streams. It ranges from
southern Canada through the midwestern and southern states
into Mexico.

The bluegill gets its common name from the blue coloring on
its chin and the lower parts of its gill covers. It is greenish on the
back, silvery on the sides, and yellow below. Young individuals
and females have vertical bars on their sides. The pectoral fins
are long and pointed, and the dorsal fin has a dark spot near its
back margin. It is an excellent tasting fish that often exceeds half
a pound, making it a very desirable panfish. The state hook-
and-line record for a bluegill is 2 pounds, 13 ounces, and the
world record is 4 pounds, 12 ounces, for a specimen caught
in Ketona Lake, Alabama, in 1950.

The bluegill feeds on various small animals and plants. The
young eat mostly insects and similar organisms and add snails
and small fishes to their diet as they grow. Bluegills are most
often caught by still fishing with worms. Because bluegills'
mouths are small, the angler should use a small hook. Bluegills
also attack small artificial baits and fight gamely on light tackle.

Bluegills spawn in May and June and occasionally as late as August in Minnesota. Males clear a depression in the bottom for a nest and wait for females to enter the spawning area. After spawning, the male chases the female away and guards the eggs and the young until the young leave.

The bluegill is an important fish in farm ponds in which fishes are raised for food and sport. There the bluegill and the largemouth bass complement each other well.

Pumpkinseed, *Lepomis gibbosus* (Linnaeus)

Scientific name: *Lepomis* = scaled gill cover (Greek); *gibbosus* = wide margin (Greek).

The pumpkinseed is a very popular panfish in Minnesota, as are bluegills and crappies. It occurs along with the bluegill in lakes and streams over much of the state. Like the bluegill, the pumpkinseed is uncommon in the Lake Superior drainage, where its occurrence is perhaps due to introductions. The pumpkinseed ranges from Manitoba through eastern Canada and south into the middle and eastern United States. Its range is complementary to some southern species of sunfishes that have similar life histories.

The pumpkinseed resembles the bluegill and can usually be distinguished from the latter by the presence of an orange spot near the tip of the operculum and by the absence of a dark spot near the back of the dorsal fin. It is smaller than the bluegill in Minnesota, where its length seldom exceeds 8 inches. It is a colorful fish, grayish green on top, green on the sides, and yellow below, with vertical bars on its sides and spots of orange scattered on its scales. Its mouth is small, and its pectoral fins are long and pointed.

Pumpkinseeds feed mostly around weed beds, where they seek insects and similar small organisms, snails, and small fishes. They bite readily on worms, grasshoppers, and small artificial lures and are comparable to bluegills in their fighting qualities and tastiness.

The pumpkinseed spawns from May through June in Minnesota in nests cleared by the males in shallow, quiet water. Males guard the eggs and the young. Pumpkinseeds, bluegills, and

Pumpkinseed sunfish

green sunfish sometimes form nesting colonies together, where spawning, chasing, and guarding behavior make for an active scene. The nests can be close together, and hybridization sometimes occurs. Hybrids of pumpkinseeds and bluegills are abundant in some lakes in central Minnesota.

Longear Sunfish, *Lepomis megalotis* (Rafinesque)

Scientific name: *Lepomis* = scaled gill cover (Greek); *megalotis* = great ear (Greek).

The main part of the range of the longear sunfish is from Mexico northward and eastward through the mideastern United States to Quebec. It is known in Minnesota from only two places, Little Rock Lake in Morrison County and Hustler Lake in St. Louis County, both of which are well separated from each other and from the main range. Only one specimen was taken at each of these two places. An isolated population of longear sunfish is also known from Lake Burditt in southern Ontario, north of Minnesota. The occurrence of the longear sunfish in these locations is curious and could be natural or the result of recent introductions. Those who studied the population in Lake Burditt have suggested that its occurrence there is natural, albeit far from the central range.

The longear sunfish owes its common name to the distinctly developed lobe that extends back from the rear of the operculum. This lobe is larger than that of other Minnesota sunfishes. The longear sunfish is very colorful, with its back and sides bluish and green flecked with yellow and orange, its belly yellow, its fins orange, and its cheeks marked with blue streaks. Breeding males are especially bright. The longear sunfish's pectoral fins are short and rounded.

The longear sunfish is similar to other sunfishes in its diet and breeding behavior. Breeding males clear nests close to each other, and females spawn in more than one nest.

White Crappie, *Pomoxis annularis* Rafinesque

Scientific name: *Pomoxis* = opercle sharp (Greek); *annularis* = having rings (Latin).

The white crappie lives in lakes and streams over central and southern Minnesota, apparently reaching the northern limits of its natural range in the Mississippi River system in the state. It is known from the Red River drainage in Minnesota, where it is uncommon, suggesting that it was possibly introduced there. It is locally common in lakes in southern Minnesota and in backwaters of the Mississippi, Minnesota, and St. Croix rivers and their tributaries. It ranges from Minnesota east into Ontario and south through the Midwest to the Gulf of Mexico.

The white crappie typically reaches a weight of between 1 and 2 pounds in Minnesota. It is green on top and silvery to white on the sides and belly, with dark vertical bars on the sides. Although the white crappie is usually paler than the black crappie, the two species resemble each other closely enough that one should not always rely on color to distinguish them. The most reliable distinguishing characteristic is the length of the dorsal fin, which is shorter in the white crappie than in the black crappie. In the white crappie, the distance from the front of the dorsal fin to the eye is distinctly greater than the length of the fin itself; in the black crappie, the distance from the front of the dorsal fin to the eye and the length of the fin itself are about equal. Also, the white crappie usually has only six spines in the dorsal fin, and the black crappie has seven or eight, although this trait is variable.

The white crappie eats a variety of small aquatic animals, including small fishes. Crappies are popular game and food fishes in Minnesota and are caught most readily on small minnows. They also bite on worms and artificial lures.

White crappies spawn from May through June in Minnesota. Males clear depressions in the bottom in shallow water for nests and guard the eggs and the young that hatch.

Black Crappie, *Pomoxis nigromaculatus* (LeSueur)

Scientific name: *Pomoxis* = opercle sharp (Greek); *nigromaculatus* = black spotted (Latin).

The black crappie is common in streams and small- to medium-size lakes over much of Minnesota except the deep, rocky lakes of the northeast. Its distribution is similar to, but wider than, that of the white crappie, ranging from Canada south through the Midwest and most of the eastern United States, including Florida. It is a more important fish in Minnesota than the white crappie because it is more abundant and widespread.

The black crappie reaches a weight of a pound or more in Minnesota. It is green above and white below. Its silvery sides are marked with distinct black and green patches. The black crappie has a longer dorsal fin than the white crappie and usual-

Black crappie

ly has seven or eight spines in the dorsal fin, in contrast to the white crappie's six.

The food habits of the black crappie are similar to those of the white crappie, and it, too, is most readily caught on minnows, worms, and small artificial lures. Black crappies often swim together in schools, and the fishing is good for the angler who happens onto a school. One reason that crappies (especially black crappies) are important to Minnesota anglers is that they are much more active in the winter than the state's other sunfishes, and the crappies are by far the most common panfishes caught at that time of year. People ice fishing usually catch them on minnows in water 10 to 15 feet deep near drop-offs.

The black crappie spawns in May and June in Minnesota. The male clears a nest that he subsequently guards. Female crappies produce eggs in prolific quantities. As with other sunfishes, populations of stunted crappies can develop where they are not controlled, and some lakes in central and southern Minnesota contain populations of stunted crappies today. An important method of panfish management used by the Minnesota DNR is thinning out the populations of stunted panfishes in lakes where they occur and releasing the captured fishes into other lakes where there is adequate room and food for them. When reduced in numbers or released into new, favorable environments, stunted panfishes resume their normal rates of growth so that the populations in both donor and recipient lakes benefit.

Family PERCIDAE
The Perches

The perch family includes the second-largest number of species in northern fresh waters; it ranks second to the minnow family. The family Percidae includes the well-known state fish of Minnesota, the walleye, the less well known sauger, and the ubiquitous perch. The family also includes a group of small and diverse fishes known as the darters, which some people might confuse with minnows or small game fishes. The family is composed of three quite distinct groups of fishes: the common perch in the subfamily Percinae, the walleye and the sauger in the subfamily Luciopercinae, and the darters in the subfamily Etheostominae.

The darters are found only in North America and originally were found only east of the Rocky Mountains. Members of the Etheostominae are among the most fascinating of all North American fishes, and 15 species live in Minnesota waters. Prof. Stephen A. Forbes, of the University of Illinois, in 1884 described the ecological role and the nature of the subfamily of darters as follows: "Given a supply of certain kinds of foods nearly inaccessible to the ordinary fish, it is to be expected that some fishes will become especially fitted for its utilization. Thus *Etheostoma* is to be explained by the hypothesis of the progressive adaptation of the young of certain Percinae to a peculiar place of refuge and a peculiarly situated food supply. These are the mountaineers among fishes. Forced from the populous and fertile valleys of the river beds and lake bottoms, they have taken refuge from their enemies in the rocky highlands, where the free waters play in careless torrents, and there they have wrested from stubborn nature a meager living. Although diminished in size by their constant struggle with the elements, they have an activity and hardihood, a vigor of life and a glow of high color, almost unknown among the easier livers of the lower lands. Notwithstanding their trivial size, they do not seem dwarfed so much as concentrated fishes."

The American pioneer of ichthyology David Starr Jordan, naturalist, educator, and statesman, wrote about one species of darter, the Johnny darter, in 1888: "Any one who has ever been a boy and can remember back to the days of tag-alders, yellow cowslips, and an angleworm on a pinhook, will recall an experience like this: You tried some time to put your finger on a little fish that was lying, apparently asleep, on the bottom of the stream, half hidden under a stone or leaf, his tail bent around the stone, as if for support against the force of the current. You will remember that when your finger came near the spot where he was lying, the bent tail straightened, and you saw the fish resting, head upstream, a few feet away, leaving you puzzled to know whether you had seen the movement or not. You were trying to catch a Johnny darter. Nothing seems easier, but you did not do it." Many readers have probably watched either a Johnny darter or an Iowa darter while they were sitting on a dock and looking into the shallows or musing at a river's edge. There is little that can be added to Jordan's description. The darters are truly unique, truly North American pioneers, perhaps the most fascinating of all American fishes.

Yellow Perch, *Perca flavescens* (Mitchill)

Scientific name: *Perca* = early Greek name for perch; *flavescens* = yellow (Latin).

The yellow perch can reach a length of 12 to 15 inches and weigh more than a pound. Its body is usually yellow on the sides, with six to eight crossbands that extend from the back to slightly below the middle of the sides. The coloration, however, can vary considerably from a very pale yellow to a bright orangish yellow. The dorsal fins are pigmented with black, and in adults the membranes between the last four spines are more heavily pigmented. The paired ventral fins are yellowish orange, and in breeding males the pigmentation is a more intense reddish orange. The jaws bear small teeth but no large canine, or tearing, teeth; the absence of canine teeth can be used to distinguish yellow perch from young walleyes and saugers. Young perch can be distinguished from darters by the very large serrations, or sawtoothlike structures, on the sides of their heads.

Yellow perch are predaceous and prefer a diet of minnows, but they also feed on aquatic insects, the young of other fishes, snails, leeches, and crayfish. They are diurnal fish, active in the littoral zone where rooted aquatic plants are found; but in the early evening they may move out to the open water to feed. At night they are inactive and usually rest on the bottom among the rooted vegetation. Perch travel in schools composed of individuals of the same size and age; such schools can contain thousands of individuals.

Yellow perch

Yellow perch spawn in early May in southern waters and in mid-May or early June in more-northern lakes. Spawning activity is temperature sensitive and usually begins when the water temperatures reach 45° F. Most of the spawning takes place at night. The eggs are laid in a gelatinous, ribbonlike, folded or plaited band a few inches wide. The band can be several feet long and contain 10,000 to 48,000 eggs, depending on the size of the female. A few weeks after spawning occurs, the eggs hatch and the larvae disperse and begin to feed on microscopic plants and animals. The shallow waters of many lakes in June may be filled with cloudlike schools of perch fry, which disperse out into the open parts of the lake. It is evident that the yellow perch has a high reproductive potential. If the fry are not eaten by larger fishes, such as the walleye, northern pike, and burbot, yellow perch will increase in numbers and may eventually literally take over the lake. Such perch-bound lakes result from an imbalance of the large predator–perch ratio in favor of the perch. Selective fishing for the more desirable predaceous species only tips the balance farther and favors a further increase in the numbers of perch and eventually in a stunting of the individuals composing the perch population. To the angler, the small perch seem a nuisance. A hundred small perch may be the equivalent in weight to a medium-size walleye or northern pike but not in the eyes of the angler. The lake then develops a reputation for being a "perch lake." Eventually, perhaps because of decreased fishing, the predators may once again increase their numbers and reduce the perch population to a level at which sportfishing quality is reestablished. More often, however, the lake does not recover, and more drastic measures must be taken. If the lake is relatively small, it can be poisoned and later restocked with game species, excluding the perch, in proportions favorable for excellent fishing. Large lakes rarely experience such perch problems, and in those lakes the perch are large and more acceptable to anglers.

The yellow perch is an excellent food fish, rivaling the walleye in quality. In fact, on the commercial market perch command a higher price per pound than walleyes do. The Red Lake Band of Chippewa Indians operates a tribal commercial fishery on Lower Red Lake that harvests an average of 212,300 pounds of perch a year.

The yellow perch has been introduced so widely in North America that it is difficult to ascertain its original distribution, which was probably from southern Canada south to Kansas and northern Missouri and east to Pennsylvania. The area from Nova Scotia south to the Carolinas in the Atlantic drainage is now included in its range. It is found throughout Minnesota, including Lake Superior and the trout streams of the North Shore.

Sauger, *Stizostedion canadense* (Smith)

Scientific name: *Stizostedion* = pungent throat (according to its author); *canadense* = of Canada.

The sauger is a slender fish, usually less than 18 inches long, that weighs 1 or 2 pounds and rarely 3 pounds. The world record for a hook-and-line-caught sauger is an 8-pound, 12-ounce, specimen caught in Lake Sakakawea in North Dakota in 1975. The Minnesota record is 6 pounds, 2½ ounces.

The sauger is grayish or blackish, with a slight brassy tinge and black blotches on its sides. The spiny dorsal fin has black spots or blotches on the membranes between the spines, and the spots form oblique rows when the fin is erect. A black spot is usually present at the base of the pectoral fin, but in some individuals the spot is not prominent, and it sometimes fades in

Sauger

dead fish. The tail fin is forked and has a thin white or creamyish streak on the ventral margin.

The sauger is primarily a river or river-lake species. It is widely distributed throughout the Mississippi River drainage from southern Arkansas to the Missouri and Ohio river basins and the Red River, from Manitoba to New Brunswick, southward to Tennessee. In Minnesota, it is common in Rainy Lake, Lake of the Woods, and Lake Kabetogama. It is also common in the St. Croix River south of Taylors Falls, the Minnesota River, and the Mississippi River south of St. Anthony Falls. Saugers are not known from the St. Louis River or the western end of Lake Superior.

Walleye, *Stizostedion vitreum* (Mitchill)

Scientific name: *Stizostedion* = pungent throat (according to its author); *vitreum* = glass (Latin), referring to the eyes.

The walleye ranges in weight from 2 to 10 pounds, but there are records of individuals weighing more than 16 pounds. The

Walleye

world record for a hook-and-line walleye is a 25-pound specimen caught in Old Hickory Lake, Tennessee, in 1960. The Minnesota record is 17 pounds, 8 ounces.

The color of the walleye varies from a dark silver to dark olive brown. Walleyes and saugers are so similar that competent biologists at times experience difficulty identifying individual fish. The late Prof. Samuel Eddy, a distinguished naturalist, biologist, and ichthyologist, once told a story about his experience with walleyes and saugers to one of his classes. During the late 1930s, while he was serving as supervisor of fisheries research for the state of Minnesota, a survey of the Rainy River and Rainy Lake was carried out and a large number of walleyes and saugers were collected. The fishes were sorted into piles of walleyes, saugers, and "questionables"; when the sorting was completed, the three piles were almost equal in size. Someone in Professor Eddy's class suggested that the questionable ones could have been the "test specimens for the next fish quiz in ichthyology." The good professor saw little humor in that comment, but he was unable to identify the humorist in his large class. Fortunately, in most instances, one does not experience the difficulty that the survey crew did. When freshly caught, walleyes display a prominent, large, black spot at the base of the last three spines of the first dorsal fin; saugers have many black spots that form oblique rows on the membranes of the spiny dorsal fin but they lack the large, dark blotch at the base of the fin. The walleye lacks the dark blotch at the base of the pectoral fin that is usually present on the sauger. These characteristics are useful in fresh specimens, but the pigmentation fades quickly in dead fish. The ventral lobe of the tail fin has a prominent white margin in the walleye; the tail fin of the sauger has only a very narrow, white margin. Both species have large canine teeth. There is always a question about the existence of hybrids between the two species, but to date there is no evidence that the two ever hybridize.

Walleyes are abundant in large lakes that cover thousands of acres. They thrive in Mille Lacs, Lake Winnibigoshish, Leech Lake, Otter Tail Lake, Basswood Lake, Lake Saganaga, Gull Lake, and others. Walleyes are also found in smaller lakes, but the populations in such lakes do not seem to thrive (perhaps because of a lack of spawning sites and food) and must be augmented by stocking programs.

Many such stocking programs are carried out cooperatively by various lake associations and DNR fisheries management personnel and have been tremendously successful in reestablishing walleye populations in fished-out lakes. The process usually follows this course. The fish committee of a lake association locates small ponds near the lake that are suitable for walleye fry, and the DNR biologists then supply the fry for stocking the pond. The number of fry stocked per acre is determined by the fishery biologist and is based on years of experience. This experience helps ensure that the fry will not be crowded and compete with one another. The pond produces an abundant supply of food organisms, and, in the absence of other fishes, the walleye fry grow rapidly, more rapidly than in a usual lake setting. In the late autumn, the fingerlings are trapped, weighed, and planted by the fisheries workers and association members in their lake or lakes. Records are kept of the number of fingerlings stocked (based on numbers per pound), and the productivity and survival rates of walleye fry in various ponds are ascertained. During subsequent years, the stocked lake is test-netted to determine the success or failure of the stocking effort. In many studies, the fins of the stocked fingerlings are clipped so that they can be easily separated from fingerlings produced by the resident walleye population. Using various fin combinations, it is possible to keep track of each year's stocking and its contribution to the population.

The results of these cooperative efforts have, in many instances, been dramatic, and walleye fishing has been restored to levels recalled by the old-timers. The rearing ponds may be fertilized occasionally to increase the potential production of food for the walleye fry. Many of the lake associations also have made great efforts to improve the water quality of their lakes, have cleaned out barriers in streams where walleyes may spawn, and have helped restrict poaching during the spawning run, when the walleyes are extremely vulnerable to illicit netting and spearing. The spirit of cooperation exhibited is to be applauded and encouraged.

The walleye has a wide distribution in North America, from

the Northwest Territories across Canada east of the Rocky Mountains to Labrador, southward along the Atlantic Coast to North Carolina, west to Arkansas, and north along the Missouri River. The walleye may be the most desirable warm-water game fish, and it has been widely introduced through North America. It has become an important species in the thousands of reservoirs throughout the western and southern United States. In Minnesota, the walleye was native to many lakes and streams throughout the state, and, where it was absent, it has been introduced.

The walleye is the most sought after of all Minnesota game fishes, and it is the mainstay of the sport fishery of the state. It is only fitting that it was selected as the state fish by the Minnesota legislature. Although long considered to be Minnesota's most popular fish, the walleye did not become the legally designated state fish until 1965. On April 26 of that year, State Representatives Keith Hinman of Grey Eagle, Leonard R. Dickinson of Bemidji, William J. O'Brien of St. Paul, B. F. DuBois of Sauk Centre, and John A. Hartle of Owatonna introduced House File No. 2044, "a bill for an act designating the walleye as the official state fish." This bill was passed by the House by a vote of 128 to 1 on May 5, passed by the Senate by a vote of 52 to 3 on May 15, and signed into law by Governor Karl F. Rolvaag on May 21. In this way, the walleye officially assumed its place, so long given it by anglers, as Minnesota's leading game fish.

Crystal Darter, *Ammocrypta asprella* (Jordan)

Scientific name: *Ammocrypta* = sand concealed (Greek); *asprella* = from *Aspro*, a European genus of perch.

The crystal darter is usually less than 5 inches long. Its body is slender and elongate, and its **standard length** is at least seven times as great as its body depth. Its flesh is almost translucent, and there are three to seven saddlelike blotches over the fish's back. There are four to six black blotches on its sides.

The crystal darter ranges from southeastern Minnesota to southern Ohio and south to Alabama and Oklahoma. It is extremely rare in Minnesota, and the authors' recent collections of the fish are from the Zumbro River near Kellogg. The habitat of this darter is in the shelter of old driftwood and stumps that are partially buried in a shifting sand bottom. Specimens can be collected by stretching out a seine downstream from an old stump or log and then kicking around the base of the obstruction to dislodge any fish that are present. The current carries the fish into the seine, and the seine is quickly taken out of the stream. A seine with a center bag is useful for this sampling technique. Little is known about the biology of this darter.

Western sand darter

Western Sand Darter, *Ammocrypta clara* Jordan and Meek

Scientific name: *Ammocrypta* = sand concealed (Greek); *clara* = clear (Latin).

The western sand darter is a slender fish that reaches a length of about 2½ inches. A living sand darter is almost transparent, but after preservation this darter displays a series of small, square blotches along its sides and many oblong, dark olive spots on the dorsal midline.

The sand darter ranges from the southern half of Minnesota to Indiana and south to eastern Texas. Its habitat is shifting sand bottom in moderate to swift current, as the generic name suggests. When disturbed, the little darter enters the loose sand and becomes concealed from sight.

A common associate of the sand darter is the translucent, speckled chub, *Hybopsis aestivalis*. The two species are common in the Minnesota River, the St. Croix River south of Taylors Falls, the Mississippi River south of St. Anthony Falls, and the lower reaches of the Cannon and Zumbro rivers.

Log perch

Log Perch, *Percina caprodes* (Rafinesque)

Scientific name: *Percina* = little perch;
caprodes = resembling a pig (Greek), referring to the snout.

The log perch is a large darter that reaches a length of about 6 inches. The body is yellowish brown or straw color in life. There are up to 19 vertical, brownish crossbars or bands that run along the sides. The number of bands is variable and ranges from 9 to 19, usually 15 or 16. In some populations, the crossbars may be vague and look like blotches. The log perch has a prominent black spot at the base of its tail fin. One of the more striking features of this darter is its broad head, which tapers to a piglike snout that overhangs the mouth. Log perch, particularly small individuals, are sometimes mistaken for small yellow perch or walleyes, which they superficially resemble.

The log perch ranges from Saskatchewan to Quebec and south to Texas and western Florida. It is common in lakes and streams throughout Minnesota and is the only member of the genus *Percina* in the state found in lakes.

Gilt Darter, *Percina evides* (Jordan and Copeland)

Scientific name: *Percina* = little perch;
evides = attractive (Greek).

The gilt darter is a handsome little fish found in the St. Croix River and its tributaries from Stillwater northward. The breeding male is brightly colored, with yellowish orange on its breast and head; its back is blackish. The female is a more subdued olive or bronze color, with seven or eight bands across its back. In males, the bands remain evident after breeding has been completed, and the spaces between the bands are filled with yellowish or reddish blotches. The first dorsal fin has 10 to 13 spines, with dark pigment on the membranes between the spines and a dark reddish orange band on the fin margin. The second dorsal fin, with 13 soft rays, is lightly pigmented. The anal fin has two spines and 9 to 11 soft rays, and it is unpigmented.

Very little is known about the natural history of this small fish, but a study of its life history is currently being undertaken. One interesting observation the authors have made is that the gilt darter spends more time actively swimming than do other native Minnesota darters. In an aquarium, the gilt darters are usually active, and they rest only occasionally on the bottom; other species of darters generally perch on their paired fins on the bottom and dart from place to place.

Seventy years ago, the gilt darter was present in the Cannon River, a tributary of the Mississippi River just north of Red Wing, Minnesota. Intensive collecting in the Cannon River from Welch to the mouth has failed to produce any additional specimens. It would appear that the gilt darter population in the St. Croix River is either a modern relic or a separate segment of a once-continuous population that included the Ohio River drain-

Male gilt darter

age east to New York and the lower Mississippi River south to Oklahoma and Georgia.

The clear-water habitat of the gilt darter has been eliminated by siltation in southeastern Minnesota; the boulder-rubble bottoms of many of those streams are now buried beneath several feet of sand and silt. One can only speculate that the habitat modification that accompanied the development of intensive agriculture and the soil erosion associated with it contributed to the disappearance of this attractive little fish. Fortunately, the designation of the St. Croix River as a Wild and Scenic River and the past restricted use of the land adjacent to the river by the Northern States Power Company should assure the survival of the gilt darter in Minnesota waters.

Blackside darter

Blackside Darter, *Percina maculata* (Girard)

Scientific name: *Percina* = little perch; *maculata* = spotted (Latin).

The blackside darter reaches a maximum length of about 3 inches. Its body is greenish yellow, with a prominent black band on the sides formed by seven to nine confluent blotches. The blotches never form vertical bars. The fish's head is pointed and elongate.

The blackside darter ranges from Saskatchewan and North Dakota to New York and southward to Alabama and Oklahoma.

It is common in the Mississippi River drainage below St. Anthony Falls, the Minnesota River, the St. Croix River below Taylors Falls, and the Red River drainage, including the Rainy River. The preferred habitat of the blackside darter is streams and small rivers, such as the Cottonwood, Otter Tail, Des Moines, and Zumbro rivers.

Slenderhead Darter, *Percina phoxocephala* (Nelson)

Scientific name: *Percina* = little perch; *phoxocephala* = slender head (Greek).

The slenderhead darter reaches a length of 3 to 4 inches and is the most slender and elongate of all the species of the genus *Percina* found in Minnesota waters. Its body is a yellowish brown, with 10 to 12 narrow, dark bands or blotches on the sides along the lateral line; these bands may be confluent, giving the appearance of a black lateral band. The male is more colorful than the female. The first dorsal fin of the male has a reddish orange band in the middle on the membrane and a pale blue or dark blue outer margin.

The slenderhead darter ranges from Minnesota to western Pennsylvania and south to Oklahoma and Tennessee. It was not until 1943 when Dr. Raymond Johnson and Dr. John Moyle collected specimens from the Root River that ichthyologists be-

Slenderhead darter

came aware that the slenderhead darter was present in Minnesota waters. A decade later, the authors became aware of the true abundance of the species in the St. Croix and Minnesota rivers, as well as in the southeastern portion of Minnesota. It is amazing that a fish so common in tributaries of these major rivers could have escaped detection for so long. Perhaps the failure can be explained by the inadequate sampling of the tributaries in the early surveys. The early surveys were concerned primarily with the economic value of Minnesota's large streams — including the main channels of the Minnesota, St. Croix, and Mississippi rivers — as sources for clams to supply the flourishing button industry of the late 1890s and early 1900s. It seems very unlikely that the slenderhead darter only recently entered Minnesota waters, for Dr. Willard Greene collected a few specimens in a tributary of the St. Croix River in Wisconsin in 1935.

River Darter, *Percina shumardi* (Gírard)

Scientific name: *Percina* = little perch; *shumardi* = named for Dr. G. C. Shumard, a surgeon with the United States Pacific Railroad Survey.

The river darter reaches a maximum length of about 3 inches. Its body is olive brown, with 9 or 10 transverse bars on the sides; the first 4 or 5 bars are narrower than the next 4 or 5 bars, which are more prominent and square shaped. There is a tear-shaped bar beneath the eye. The most useful characteristic for identification is the pigment pattern on the spiny, or first, dorsal fin. There is a black blotch on the membrane between the first and second spines and a black spot on each segment of the membranes connecting the last three spines.

The river darter ranges from Manitoba to Ohio and south to Alabama and Texas. As its common name implies, it is an inhabitant of large rivers and river lakes. River darters are common in the mouths of large streams tributary to large rivers, such as the Cannon and the Zumbro. The authors have not collected it from the Minnesota River or from the Mississippi River above St. Anthony Falls. It is absent from the Lake Superior drainage, but it is present in the Red River and Rainy River drainages, including Lake of the Woods.

This attractive little fish is named for its discoverer, Dr. G. C. Shumard, a surgeon associated with the United States Pacific Railroad Survey. During the eighteenth and nineteenth centuries, it was usual for the surgeon associated with an expedition of exploration or a survey to serve also as its naturalist. Training for the medical and natural sciences was not greatly different.

Johnny Darter, *Etheostoma nigrum* Rafinesque

Scientific name: *Etheostoma* = from *etheo*, meaning to filter, and *stoma*, meaning mouth (Greek); *nigrum* = black (Latin).

The Johnny darter is one of the more common darters native to the Midwest. It is small, usually less than 3 inches long. Johnny darters are easily recognized by the W-shaped marks on the sides of their bodies. The body of the fish is tan to dark brown, with a slight speckling of dark brown spots; the fins are flecked with brownish black spots.

Johnny darters are found in lakes and running waters, occurring in small streams and large rivers. They are generalists among the specialists; most darters are quite specialized and restricted in their habits and habitat preferences. Johnny darters can be seen perched on rocks or in patches of sand near docks;

Johnny darter

on small rocks in trout streams; adjacent to large boulders in the St. Croix, Rainy, and Kawishiwi rivers; on deadhead logs in the Minnesota River; or on the riprap of wing dams on the Mississippi River. The brown color and the W-shaped marks disrupt the outline of the Johnny darters, and they blend in so nicely with their background that only when they dart do they become visible to the casual observer.

Johnny darters spawn in May and June in nests prepared by the males under sticks, stones, and clam shells. The eggs are adhesive, and the males tend the nests and the eggs until the young hatch. The young are then left to fend for themselves. It is surprising what artifacts Johnny darters use as nesting sites — pop cans, pop bottles, old crockery, mason jars, tobacco cans, and pipe supports for docks. One might be startled to see a male darter aggressively defending an aluminum can. Johnny darters and other species of fishes can truly be adaptable.

The Johnny darter ranges from southern Canada through the upper Mississippi Valley, the Great Lakes drainage, and the Atlantic drainage southward to Florida and Arkansas.

Bluntnose Darter, *Etheostoma chlorosomum* (Hay)

Scientific name: *Etheostoma* = from *etheo,* meaning to filter, and *stoma,* meaning mouth (Greek);
chlorosomum = greenish yellow (Greek).

The bluntnose darter closely resembles the Johnny darter in coloration and size; it is usually less than 3 inches in total length. There are two distinguishing features that serve to separate the two fishes: the bluntnose darter has an incomplete lateral line that extends only to below the end of the first dorsal fin, but the Johnny darter has a complete lateral line; the bluntnose darter has a bar that extends from one eye around the tip of the snout to the other eye, but the Johnny darter has a bar that is interrupted at the tip of the snout.

The bluntnose darter is known from the Root River drainage in extreme southeastern Minnesota and the Mississippi River south of Wabasha. It ranges eastward to Indiana and southward to Alabama and Texas.

Male Iowa darter

Iowa Darter, *Etheostoma exile* (Girard)

Scientific name: *Etheostoma* = from *etheo*, meaning to filter, and *stoma*, meaning mouth (Greek); *exile* = slim (Latin).

The Iowa darter is the most common darter in the lakes of central and northern Minnesota. It is a slender fish that reaches a maximum length of about 2½ inches. The male is brightly colored, with greenish blue and brown blotches and with red spots on the sides. Female Iowa darters are brownish gray and lack bright pigments. Both sexes have a prominent black bar immediately below the eye.

The Iowa darter ranges from Saskatchewan to Quebec, southward through Colorado and the lake region of Iowa and eastward to Ohio. In Minnesota, it is the most common darter in both the lakes and the streams of the Boundary Waters Canoe Area, but in central and southern Minnesota it is restricted to the lake habitat. Occasionally, it is found in the streams and rivers connecting chains of lakes, such as the Otter Tail and Crow Wing rivers. The floodplain lakes and sloughs of the Mississippi River south of Hastings also support populations of Iowa darters.

The Iowa darter and the Johnny darter are the species of darters most commonly observed by anglers, boaters, and canoeists. The male Iowa darter is the most obvious darter because of its spectacular coloration.

Mud darter

Mud Darter, *Etheostoma asprigene* (Forbes)

Scientific name: *Etheostoma* = from *etheo*, meaning to filter, and *stoma*, meaning mouth (Greek); *asprigene* = from *Aspro*, a European genus of perch, and *genos*, for race (Greek).

The mud darter reaches a length of about 2½ inches. Its body is stout, rather than slender, and compressed. It is brownish in color, with greenish crossbars or blotches and reddish orange pigment between the blotches. Its belly is orangish in color. The first dorsal fin has a narrow, bluish margin, and the upper half of the fin is speckled with reddish orange. The other fins, including the second dorsal fin, are a mottled brown.

The mud darter ranges from Minnesota to Indiana and south to Mississippi and Texas. In Minnesota, it is present in the Mississippi River south of Hastings and in the St. Croix River below Taylors Falls. It is found most often in the mouths of streams tributary to the Mississippi River.

Rainbow Darter, *Etheostoma caeruleum* Storer

Scientific name: *Etheostoma* = from *etheo*, meaning to filter, and *stoma*, meaning mouth (Greek); *caeruleum* = blue (Latin).

The rainbow darter reaches a length of about 3 inches. It is a stout-bodied darter with a large head and large eyes. The rainbow darter, as the common name implies, is one of the more colorful species. In fact, breeding males may display all the col-

Male rainbow darter

Female rainbow darter

ors of the spectrum. The fish's body is olive colored, with blotches of dark olive on the back and upper body. There are about 12 bars of indigo blue that extend downward and backward. The spaces between the bars are brilliant orange, and the chest is orangish red. The first dorsal fin has blue and orange horizontal bars. The females are a subdued brownish gray color on their bodies and fins.

Rainbow darters inhabit clear, rapid waters free of domestic pollution, but they seem tolerant of average levels of agricultural enrichment. The rainbow darter is one of the more common species of darters in the small rivers and streams of southeastern Minnesota. It adapts well to life in an aquarium, despite the fact that its preferred habitat is the swift water of riffles and rapids.

The rainbow darter ranges from southern Minnesota to eastern Ontario and south to Alabama and Arkansas. In Minnesota, it is common in the Otter Tail River and the tributaries of the Minnesota River west of Mankato and in the Cannon, Zumbro, Root, and Cedar rivers in the southeastern part of the state.

Banded darter

Banded Darter, *Etheostoma zonale* (Cope)

Scientific name: *Etheostoma* = from *etheo*, meaning to filter, and *stoma*, meaning mouth (Greek); *zonale* = banded (Latin).

The banded darter is a slender fish with a blunt snout. The fish reaches a maximum length of about 2½ inches. It is greenish in color, with six greenish brown rectangular spots on its back. There is a greenish olive band on its sides from which eight narrow, green bands extend and nearly or completely encircle the belly. The fins are greenish or yellowish green, and in the male the first dorsal fin has a basal band of dark red pigment.

The banded darter inhabits swift water in gravel-rubble riffles and rapids. It is quite often an associate of the rainbow darter. The banded darter ranges from southern Minnesota to Ohio and western New York and south to Alabama and Oklahoma. In Minnesota, it is most common in the tributaries of the Mississippi River south of Hastings and in the Cannon, Zumbro, and Root river drainages. It has also been taken from the tributaries of the Minnesota River west of Mankato.

Male fantail darter

Female fantail darter

Fantail Darter, *Etheostoma flabellare* Rafinesque

Scientific name: *Etheostoma* = from *etheo*, meaning to filter, and *stoma*, meaning mouth (Greek); *flabellare* = fanlike (Latin), referring to the tail.

The fantail darter reaches a maximum length of about 3 inches. Its body is heavy, and its head is quite pointed. The coloration of the fish is variable, ranging from brown to olive black to intense black. A spot on each scale gives the impression of a series of parallel lines running the length of the body. From this comes the midwestern fantail's common name, the striped fantail darter.

The fantail darter is found in streams and small rivers from Minnesota eastward to Vermont and southward to North Carolina and Oklahoma. It is common in the western tributaries of the Minnesota River and in the tributaries of the Mississippi River south of the Twin Cities.

Least darter

Least Darter, *Etheostoma microperca* Jordan and Gilbert

Scientific name: *Etheostoma* = from *etheo*, meaning to filter, and *stoma*, meaning mouth (Greek); *microperca* = small perch (Greek).

The least darter is the smallest fish known from Minnesota waters. It reaches 1 to 1½ inches in total length. These darters are so small that they are able to escape through the mesh of a 1/4-inch seine. Using 1/8- or 1/16-inch woven-mesh seines is necessary to capture least darters.

Male least darters are more colorful than female least darters, and the males have extremely long and large pectoral fins that reach back to the anus. Other than its size, the distinctive feature of this darter is the almost complete absence of a lateral line. Generally, only one to four scales in the lateral line are pored.

The habitat of the least darter is the heavily vegetated areas of small streams and lakes. Such habitats are difficult to seine, and this fact, plus the small size of the fish, have led the authors to believe that the least darter is often missed in routine sampling.

The least darter ranges from Minnesota eastward to southern Ontario and southward to Kentucky, Arkansas, and Oklahoma. In Minnesota, it is found in the Otter Tail River, the Red River drainage, the Crow Wing River and its tributaries, the Mississippi River above St. Anthony Falls, Lake Minnewaska, and Otter Creek, a tributary of the Cedar River south of Austin. This discontinuous distribution, with the isolated population in the Cedar River, is quite peculiar among Minnesota fishes, and no completely satisfactory explanation can be proposed. Perhaps biologists have not sampled extensively and intensively enough in the preferred habitat; or the habitat has been modified by human activities (lumbering, agriculture, and lake development, for example), thus reducing the populations of the least darter. The explanation must await further studies of the biology of this attractive and secretive little fish.

Family SCIAENIDAE
The Drums

The family Sciaenidae is a large group that includes the drums, sea trouts, and croakers. Only one species in this family, the freshwater drum, lives in fresh water, and Minnesota is in its range. Many of the marine drums are important food fishes. Typical members of the drum family have interesting characteristics: they have a special set of muscles that they can vibrate against the swim bladder to produce the loud drumming or croaking sound for which the family is named; the skull contains large, hardened ear bones commonly called earstones; and the lateral line runs all the way to the rear edge of the tail fin.

Freshwater Drum, *Aplodinotus grunniens* Rafinesque

Scientific name: *Aplodinotus* = simple back (Greek); *grunniens* = grunting (Latin).

The freshwater drum is found in rivers, streams, and shallow lakes over much of Minnesota except the Lake Superior drainage. It is most common in the Red River drainage and in the southern part of the state. Its range is from Canada southward through the Midwest to Guatemala.

The freshwater drum is so named because of the drumming or grunting noise it can make with its swim bladder. It is also called the sheepshead, croaker, and thunderpumper. Its back is gray, with purplish reflections, its sides are silver, and its belly is

Freshwater drum

white. It can be distinguished from all other Minnesota fishes by its lateral line, which runs through the tail fin.

The freshwater drum occasionally reaches a weight of 20 pounds in Minnesota. It usually stays near the bottom, where it forages for small fishes, immature insects, crayfish, and small clams. It has heavy pharyngeal teeth with which to grind its food (Figure 47). It sometimes bites on a hook, but it is not regarded very highly as a food fish in Minnesota. Freshwater drums caught commercially are sometimes sold as white perch.

The freshwater drum spawns in May and June in Minnesota. Spawning occurs in open water, and the eggs are shed randomly. The rumbling sound that drums make may be associated with breeding activities — at least, the sound is heard most frequently in breeding season.

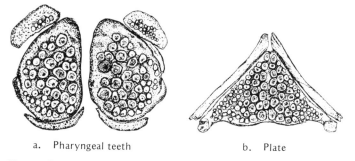

a.   Pharyngeal teeth   b.   Plate

Figure 47. Pharyngeal food-grinding structures of the freshwater drum: (a) pharyngeal teeth and (b) plate found in roof of pharynx.

Index

INDEX

(Pages on which photographs of the fishes appear are italicized.)

Gary L. Phillips, a science editor and icthyologist, received his doctorate in zoology at the University of Minnesota. Photographer William D. Schmid and James C. Underhill are professors in the department of ecology and behavioral biology at Minnesota. Underhill is co-author, with Samuel Eddy, of *Northern Fishes* and *How to Know the Freshwater Fishes*.